CHASING
ALICE

How the Life, Murder, and Legacy
of an English Teacher Changed
a Delmarva Community

Stephanie L. Fowler

First Edition

ISBN 978-1-62806-276-2   (print | paperback)
ISBN 978-1-62806-277-9   (print | hardback)
ISBN 978-1-62806-278-6   (ebook)
ISBN 978-1-62806-279-3   (ebook)

Library of Congress Control Number 2020907962

Published by Salt Water Media
29 Broad Street, Suite 104
Berlin, MD 21811
www.saltwatermedia.com

Printed in the United States.

Cover design and maps by Brian Robertson of Brian Robertson Designs. The image of Alice is from the Parsons family collection. Author photo by Kelly O'Brien Russo of Kelly Russo Photography. Interior layout by Salt Water Media.

Author website: www.stephaniefowler.net

CHASING
ALICE

Alice Parsons Davis Memorial Scholarship
The Community Foundation of the Eastern Shore
1324 Belmont Avenue, Suite 401
Salisbury, Maryland 21804
www.cfes.org

•   •   •   •   •

The National Domestic Violence Hotline
(800) 799-7233
(800) 787-3224 for TTY
www.thehotline.org

To Alice

· · · · ·

And to those who love her and remember her.

And to those who may hear her story
and make a change before it is too late.

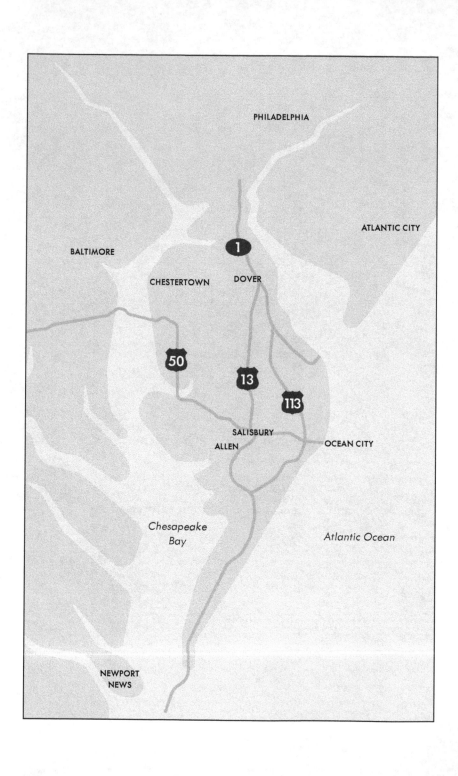

"The web of our life is of a mingled yarn,
good and ill together."

All's Well That Ends Well, Act IV, Scene iii

• • • • •

Table of Contents

Part II

Part III

Part IV

Part V

Acknowledgments

This book would not exist without the kindness, help, and dedication of many people.

I am deeply appreciative of Alice's family for helping me with this project, especially her sisters. Barrie Parsons Tilghman and Ellen Malone Hitch provided me with invaluable information about Alice and their family, including old family photos. I know the interviews were sometimes difficult, but Barrie and Ellen were always open and honest with me. I admired their candidness, which I can only assume was a lot like having Mary Belle in the room.

I am forever grateful to Lori Lopez. Honestly, I was the most nervous about approaching her, but I quickly discovered that Lori is an amazing person, full of strength and hope and love. She spoke with me several times, and without her, this book would have been incomplete. I wish I could put into words my gratitude to Lori and my respect for her perseverance.

I would like to thank Patricia Slocum who spoke with me early in the research phase.

Alice's fellow teachers were of enormous help to me: Cindy Bennett, Anne Collins, Colleen Dallam, Dawn Neville, and Aimee Orme. These women taught me while I was at Parkside and Anne Collins is still giving me homework and reading assignments even now. It took me a little while to get comfortable calling them by their first names, proof that old habits are hard to break. They were wonderful to me and so accommodating as I picked my way through their photographs, documents, and most importantly, their memories of Alice. These kind of conversations are never easy, but through talking with these incredible women, I gained a new perspective on Alice and I could not have done this work without Cindy, Anne, Colleen, Dawn, and Aimee.

Also in that Parkside crew, I have to thank Micah Stauffer for granting me an interview and sharing his remembrances, speeches, and emails from that time in his tenure.

One of my favorite interviews for this book happened when I sat down with Gale Glasgow Dashiell. She had some of the sweetest and most charming memories of Alice. Gale and I had several conversations after the initial interview and she was so quick to help clarify or dig a little deeper into her memory bank whenever I had a question. Gale was always kind and compassionate to me and I won't forget it.

I sent Matthew Collier a letter, asking him if he might be willing to do an interview with me. I knew it was a big ask, and after a year went by, I figured the answer was no. But one day, out of the blue, I got an email from him and I was so glad I did. Matthew's insight shaped key parts of the project for me.

Alice's friends and neighbors, Marisa Carey and her partner, Maria, welcomed me into their home and talked with me for several hours at their kitchen table. I learned a great deal from them.

I also must thank several of Alice former students: Tyron Corbin, Kelly Hager, Barbara Kiviat, Dixie White Leikach, Ann Lawrence Rives, Kelly Hughes Roberts, Carl Thress, Tiffany Hoke Vandervoordt, and Brooks Williams. They all shared what they remembered from their time in her class and each one spoke warmly and affectionately of Alice. It was clear how much she meant to each and every one of them.

The Wicomico County Sheriff's Office was extremely helpful to me as I researched the case files. I submitted the Freedom of Information Act / Public Information Act paperwork and 1st Sergeant Mark Wagner, Sergeant Anthony Glenn, Maureen Lanigan, and Carol Wallingford responded to my inquiries. Maureen and Carol pulled the case files and assembled a boatload of documents for me.

My sincerest thanks go directly to Sheriff Mike Lewis, Detective Sergeant Chastity Blades, and Corporal Sabrina Metzger for talking with me about the case. These interviews were instrumental in helping me understand specific law enforcement aspects of this case. Sheriff Lewis all but rolled out a red carpet for me and made every resource available to me that he could. After meeting with Blades and Metzger, I walked away with the utmost respect for them. They are extraordinary women on the front lines. The insights of Lewis, Blades, and Metzger helped shaped parts of the book and I couldn't have done it without them.

After I received the autopsy and toxicology reports from the Office of the Chief Medical Examiner in Baltimore, I realized I was going to need help in understanding them. (Quick thanks to Shea Lawson at the OCME for helping me obtain these records.) I turned to one of my dearest friends, Dr. Mithila Jegathesan. She walked me through all the terminology and medications and explained it in terms I could wrap my brain around since my medical background is limited. Mithila, or Dr. J. as she is known to her patients, is one of the smartest people I know and she is always ready to answer the call when someone needs help. I have a great admiration for her.

I would also like to thank a couple of mental health profession-als who talked with me about the dynamics of abusive relationships and domestic violence. They suggested resources and books to read and answered what questions they could. They wished to remain anonymous and I am honoring that request.

Writing is a lonely endeavor, but over the years, I have been for-tunate to find myself in the midst of a fantastic, indispensable circle of writer friends. My heart and this book owe a great debt of grat-itude to Tony Russo, Jeffrey Smith, Barbara Lockhart, Benjamin Beck, and Andrew Heller. They all read my first and second drafts and provided me feedback — good, bad, and ugly. This means they voluntarily read 400 pages of my work ... it is a big favor to ask. Hopefully, the upside is they know that I love each and every one of them. Tony pushed me to meet deadlines that I often broke and constantly reminded me to "serve the narrative!"; Jeffrey shared his good whiskey and provided deep, emotional examinations of my work; Barbara absolutely saved the entire book by talking me off a ledge when I was ready to quit; Benjamin challenged me to dig deeper and was right in doing so; and Andrew was a therapist and a cheerleader on more occasions than either of us would like to ad-mit. I'd also like to thank the whole lot of the Lower Eastern Shore Chapter of the Maryland Writers' Association with an additional thanks to Joan Cooper, Bud Scott, and Susan Ayres Wimbrow.

Bill Cecil did the technical editing on this book and I needed his critical eye on the page. He spent six hours over two days with me, going through this manuscript page by page and line by line. The hard work is trimming and polishing and this book is stronger for his efforts.

Getting the facts right in this book meant reaching out to people like George Shivers who literally wrote the book on Allen,

Maryland. It's called *Changing Times: Chronicle of Allen, Maryland, An Eastern Shore Village.* (Historians like long titles, I think.) He was also one of my professors at Washington College and is the epitome of the phrase "a gentleman and a scholar." I sent him the sections on Allen, and he offered useful notes and critical corrections.

The cover of this book brought tears to my eyes the first time I saw it. Brian Robertson, of Brian Robertson Designs, worked with me to create the perfect cover to convey how I felt about this project and Alice. Then I asked him for help with a couple of maps and he turned them right around for me. Brian is a brilliant and talented artist and our arts community is lucky to have him.

Last, but never least, I want to thank my family.

My mother, Jacki, has always encouraged and supported my writing, from the terrible poetry of my youth to the essays and stories I write now. On this book, she also held my feet to the fire. If I had a dollar for every time she asked me, "Is it done yet?" then I'd have about a bazillion dollars. (She knows I'm kidding because she knows I love her.) One of the best things to ever happen to my mother was a gentleman named Merrill Lockfaw. He came along in 2016 and although he isn't my stepfather legally, he might as well be. Merrill has helped heal a hole in my heart, for sure, and I love him to pieces. They just don't make 'em like him anymore.

My little sister, Kristen, has been proud of just about everything I have ever written in my life, even when I didn't think my work was any good. She has been my best friend since we were little kids and she has always cheered me on and fought for me. Kristen is an amazing, badass human and I love her with my whole heart. (And one kidney.)

And then there is my wife, Patty. Living with a writer cannot be easy, and I don't know how she does it. She has been on this journey with me since the very beginning. There are no words to encapsulate how much she means to me ... I only know that I am more fortunate than I should be to walk beside her every day of my life. Patty held my hand through some of the toughest parts of this work, like the heart-wrenching moment when I got the police files and the sleepless nights when I was full of self-doubt. And there were many. She helped me with computer files and research; she listened to my whining and tolerated my obsessive nature and my weird, writerly quirks. None of which, I'm sorry to say, is likely to change. This book and I owe her everything. I love her beyond all measure ... and that too is not likely to change.

Thank you.

- Stephanie L. Fowler

POSTSCRIPT: While I was writing this book, our dog, Lima, functioned as my watchful editor. I often suspected she was in cahoots with my mother, my wife, and Benjamin Beck to keep me on task. If the writing was good, Lima would nap next to my desk; if it wasn't, she'd nap under the desk and heave great sighs upward. What a pup! For her efforts, she demanded a line in this section. And extra treats.

Author's Note:
On Chasing Alice

In the winter of 2015, Netflix released a documentary called *Making A Murderer*. The ten-episode series revolved around a Wisconsin man named Steven Allan Avery who was tried and convicted of the murder of Teresa Halbach, a young photographer who went missing after a brief interaction with Avery. Because of the explosive and controversial nature of the documentary, *Making a Murderer* dominated social media and the news for weeks on end while simultaneously sparking national outcry over the treatment of Steven Avery, his family, Teresa Halbach, her family, and several others featured in the documentary. I, like nearly everyone else with a Netflix account, absorbed myself in it: the details, the personalities, the crimes, the trials, the emotions. It felt impossible to look away.

Their lives and these intimate scenes played out in front of us. I remember looking at the deep wrinkles on the face of Dolores Avery, Steven's mother, as she sat silent, broken down, in her faded housecoat at her kitchen table while a television blared from a nearby room in her trailer. The family owned a salvage yard and appeared to live a step or two above abject poverty. *This is her real life*, I kept reminding myself, and in those moments, just the passive act of viewership felt intrusive and awkward because of the underlying, inescapable sense that I had witnessed something gruesome without once averting my eyes. This is the nature of true crime: it often feels darkly voyeuristic.

Several weeks after watching the series, I came across a *New Yorker* article by Kathryn Schulz on *Making A Murderer*. There was a poignant moment in her story about the nature of the true crime genre and it made me pause. She wrote: "...Yet the most obvious thing to say about true crime documentaries is something that, surprisingly often, goes unsaid: they turn people's private tragedies into public entertainment. If you have lost someone to violent crime, you know that, other than the loss itself, few things are as painful and galling as the daily media coverage, and the license it gives to strangers to weigh in on what happened ..."

Her quote encapsulates my greatest personal struggle in writing this book.

Alice Davis was my English teacher during my senior year at Parkside High School in Salisbury, Maryland. I was in her class from September 1996 until my graduation in May 1997. During that school year, my mother was in renal failure and I was struggling. Alice was the only person who noticed I was in trouble and she mentored me through it. She recognized my passion for writing and she nurtured those aspirations in me. She challenged me and she encouraged me, and I never forgot it. I never forgot her because I loved her.

I wish the story stopped there, but it does not. On Sunday, September 4th, 2011, her husband brutally murdered her, discarded her body in the woods near Princess Anne, Maryland, and then reported her as a missing person. I wish I had the words to describe the heartbreak I felt, the grief which rooted itself inside every person who knew her and loved her. Our community was bereft and anxious. We were glued to our screens — televisions, computers, phones — as news outlets reported updates on the story. The local papers ran headlines about her disappearance next to her driver's license photograph. Our Facebook feeds were jammed with posts about her. Alice was everywhere and yet nowhere at the same time. Within hours, her story made the national news, appearing on abcnews.com, CNN, and the *Huffington Post*. There was even a thread dedicated to Alice's disappearance on the *Justice for Chandra Levy* website. Each new development was quickly followed by the opinions of complete strangers pontificating as to what had happened to her and what kind of life she must have led.

For those close to Alice, there was an additional layer of sorrow underpinning the news cycles because they knew Alice would have been absolutely mortified to know her private life was spilling onto the public stage with all these prying eyes having full view of what she had so carefully hidden. Had she lived, I couldn't even begin to imagine the humiliation she would have felt upon finding herself in the center of a circle full of strangers.

Throughout the course of writing this book, I have struggled with the singular issue of privacy — Alice's privacy. *Is this book just one more point of needless exposure? Am I wrong for doing this? What if I am just further compounding the trauma, doing more harm than good for her family and friends?* I have gone back and forth over this, agonizing in my mind and out loud, repeatedly. Alice Davis was a deeply private person, so much so that she tried to keep as many of the awful details of her life a secret from her closest friends and family.

Now I have an entire book devoted to her. Perhaps this is the biggest invasion of all and this entire project renders me little more than a hypocrite because I know she valued her privacy, and yet

I have written this manuscript about her life and her death, her secrets and her legacy. This thought has pushed me to consider quitting the project on more occasions than I wish to admit.

But something else bothers me more: when I enter her name into Google, the immediate search results are of her disappearance, her gruesome murder, the suicide of her husband who was also her killer, and the heartbroken community she left behind. When I mention her name to people, most respond similarly: "Oh yeah, isn't that the teacher who was murdered by her husband?" When I sat down with her family, her friends, her co-workers, and her students, beneath the laughter and joy their memories brought forward, there was an unmistakable mixture of emotions: sadness, confusion, frustration, anger, hurt, and most of all, a profound sense of guilt. Her name has become almost synonymous with this bittersweetness and I cannot help but think Alice would detest that more.

After beginning the research and interviews for this book, I was watching an episode of *48 Hours* on CBS. The story was about a real estate agent, Vanessa Mintz, who was murdered by her husband because he was having an affair and wanted to be free. Near the end of the episode, the reporter asked her two daughters about the legacy of their mother, and one of the daughters said something that moved me: "I want my mother to be remembered for who she was, not how she died. I want my mother to be remembered as a passionate Renaissance woman that was able to tackle the world and to be near her was to be blessed." In that moment, the conflicted voice within me began to quiet down because I felt the same way about Alice.

Yes, she was a murder victim. But she was also a daughter, a sister, a wife, a stepmother, a grandmother, a best friend, a neighbor, a teacher, and a mentor. Alice was the total of many parts and that cannot be forgotten. She had 55 years with us and I do not want that last week to be the defining moment for her life. I want a better ending for her story, but that is something that no one can give her. All I could do was write. All I could do was share what I discovered of her life and what she meant to those around her. That work is now in your hands.

In chasing Alice, I interviewed more than 30 people who knew her or the case and I searched through their memories; I devoured news accounts, police records, and personal correspondences; I have been to her hometown of Allen, Maryland, to Parkside High School, to the site where her body was found, and to her grave. In private moments, I have stared at old photographs and even talked aloud to empty rooms in a last-ditch effort that she might hear me, maybe even give me a sign one way or the other. I chased Alice for her family, for her friends, for her students, for myself, and for you, because by the time you finish reading this author's note, more than 120 people in the United States will have been physically harmed by someone they know.

I chased Alice for them too.

Part I

"... what's past is prologue..."

THE TEMPEST
ACT II, SCENE i

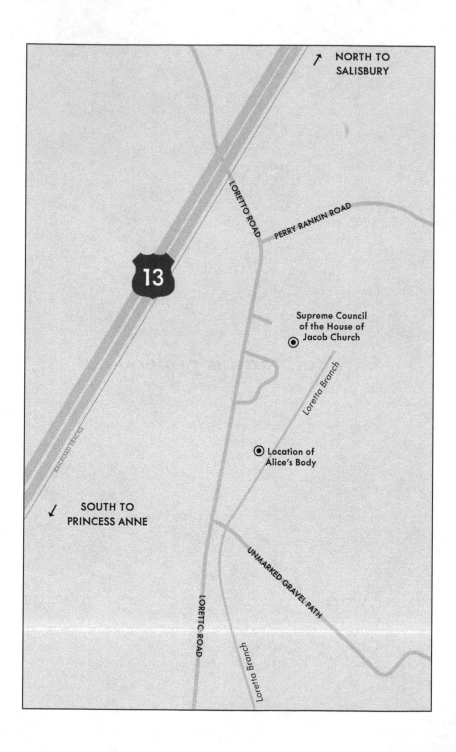

The search is over.

Loretto Road, just off Route 13 in Somerset County, Maryland, is a quiet, country road surrounded by tall forests and open fields. It is a meandering route from the village of Allen to the small town of Princess Anne on the Delmarva Peninsula, a 170-mile long stretch of land cradled between the Chesapeake Bay to its west and the Atlantic Ocean to its east. Named after the three states which comprise it — Delaware, Maryland, and Virginia — this large peninsula is a patchwork of farms, forests, and marshy flat lands, crisscrossed by countless creeks, rivers, and inlets, and peppered with cypress swamps, Mason-Dixon Line markers, and a handful of minor cities. And, as if to cap off the oddity of Delmarva, Route 13, the unluckiest of numbers, bisects it from north to south like an interminable, serpentine vein.

As country roads go, Loretto Road is unremarkable. There are no mansions or paved driveways, just ordinary rancher-style homes, farmhouses, and trailers with clamshell or stone lanes to their front doors. A copse of trees occasionally interrupts the fields between neighbors.

On its northernmost end, Loretto Road is cut by railroad tracks owned by Norfolk Southern. The line is still active, running from Porter, Delaware to Pocomoke, Maryland, and on any given day, railcars full of grain destined for chicken houses rattle and shake onward to their terminals. The poultry industry is an integral part of the agricultural commerce of the Delmarva Peninsula, and Somerset County has its share of farms. This is a rural trade: long, low-slung chicken houses hold tens of thousands of birds, seemingly uncountable numbers of warm little bodies crammed together, grown and harvested on a regular schedule. When the feces and decay combine with the humidity of summer, the result is an unforgiving stench that hangs in the air like an invisible hand of death. Sweet and sour, awful and normal: the odors and byproducts are as familiar and routine to Delmarva folks as the blue sky above and the impending changes in seasons.

Less than a mile beyond the railroad tracks, there is a white granite memorial marker, about five feet high, bearing a bronze plaque in honor of Father G. W. Israel, founding father of the Supreme Council of the House of Jacob, a non-sectarian Christian organization with a church compound on the adjoining property. The stone marker is cordoned off by a thin, black metal fence with neatly trimmed grass. The main gate is broken, but someone has tied an old USB printer cable in knots to hold the swinging doors together.

Beyond the marker is an unmarked gravel path, the entrance to an unofficial dump. Scattered among the thick clumps of American pokeweed and fragrant honeysuckle are heaps of yard trimmings and large branches, sawed off at their ends. A wooden chest of drawers lies on its side, its contents spilling outward — a shirt with thick black and white stripes, a few knock-off purses, dollar store nail polish, an empty tube of cortisone cream, and a lone purple latex glove. The gravel path parallels a small stream for several hundred yards. Almost obscured from view by overgrown weeds, the muddy brown water is an offshoot of the Loretta Branch from the Manokin River. The entire length of the path is littered with garbage: bits of broken, brown glass, half a dozen shotgun shell casings, a white and pink polka dot hair bow, a crushed soda can, and sun-bleached animal bones. Then, the path widens into an airy patch of meadow with a wide bed of low grass surrounded by Virginia pines and full maples.

It is the kind of spot that might attract lovers or conspirators, open but isolated at once.

On September 11ᵗʰ, 2011, a group of adults from the House of Jacob church were walking through those woods behind Loretto Road on their way to dispose of old party supplies in burn barrels. The heat of the lingering afternoon was beginning to break as the sun inched towards the horizon. It was just about 5 p.m. Mosquitoes nipped and roamed among the living things; bees bounced from wild flower to wild flower. The hum of insects, whether crawling in the dirt or covered under brush, ushered in the muted tones of the coming twilight. As the churchgoers approached that meadow, they came upon something strange.

At first, there was a distinct smell, akin to the chickens but more intense. Perhaps they thought it was a dead deer, evidence of negligent hunters, unwilling or unskilled enough to follow the kill to its end. Or maybe it was just an unfortunate roadkill incident. The large expanses of forest and farmland provide ample opportunity for hunters and prey alike to thrive. Hunting is a rite of a passage for the people of Delmarva, a ritual both time-honored and lucrative for the state. Larger game like white-tailed deer and Sika deer are considered valuable prizes to be photographed, mounted, field-dressed, and celebrated, but it is not uncommon for an occasional carcass to be found in a field or the woods. There are plenty of local tales of big city folks coming to the Eastern Shore to hunt wildlife, only to end up killing goats, horses and ponies, and even family dogs because they are unfamiliar with nature and her creatures from a shooting distance. A seasoned hunter would not make such a mistake, but sometimes a wounded animal does get away.

As the church group walked closer, a yellow t-shirt caught their attention. They stopped. The air was still. They stared wide-eyed at an arm and next a leg. And there in the meadow, in this place of secrecy and trash, they began to understand — they had found a dead body.

Soon after the discovery, the piercing scream of police sirens shattered the silence of the forest. One by one, police cars arrived, red and blue lights swirling, dizzying, disorienting. Metal doors slammed. Engines idled. Radios squawked. The meadow came alive as officers and detectives swarmed the spot where a caller had reported finding a body. The humidity enveloped their Kevlar-covered bodies and they recognized that unforgettable scent drifting through the trees. These woods, they knew, were about to offer up a sad secret.

And it did.

Immediately, they believed the decomposing body to be Alice Davis, the English teacher from Parkside High School who had been reported missing by her husband, Jess Henry Davis. They had been searching for her all over Somerset and Wicomico Counties for the past week, scouring farmland, forests, hunting grounds, and ditches. The clothing seemed to fit the description given in her missing persons report. An officer set to work taking photographs of the scene, juxtaposing the normal against the horrific, frame after frame: a distant view of the quiet meadow alone, a single canvas slip-on shoe in the grass, a cotton t-shirt with cartoon images of butterflies and wide-brimmed sun hats, the body, and the larvae. There was no sense to make of it, only evidence to process.

The September sun began to set around a quarter after seven that evening. The unidentified remains were placed in a black body bag and transported to Baltimore, where days later the state medical examiner's office, using dental records, confirmed everyone's suspicions. The worst fears had come to pass: the body in the woods was hers. The cause of death was listed as blunt force trauma to the head. The case was closed.

Alice was gone.

• • • •

Welcome to the Village of Allen

Allen, Maryland is a dot-on-a-map kind of place. No stoplights, only a few roads that lead in and out of a cluster of modest homes nestled among old sycamore and sassafras trees. On the edge of town, farm fields sprawl outward, reaching toward Route 13. Vines overtake telephone poles and entwine themselves around transmission lines high above the cracked asphalt. Barns, sheds, and silos in various states of neglect and disrepair stand sentinel. There is a narrow bridge over the Passerdyke Pond where the Passerdyke Creek and Wicomico Creek come together and swell like a bulging artery. Just as one might trace an ancestor, these waters bend and fork westward, flowing to the Wicomico River and the great Chesapeake Bay. The pond, dotted with lily pads and fat bullfrogs, is dark and still; the woods surrounding it are dense and rife with unseen wildlife. The thrumming heart of this place seems to exist where it cannot be seen, only sensed. As motorists enter the quaint hamlet, there is a sign nailed to a post: "Welcome to the Village of Allen 1702-2002." Just below that, another sign, knocked askew, announces that the Allen Lion's Club meets on Thursdays.

It is a time capsule of sorts, dating back to the earliest days of America when ships of European settlers and African slaves were arriving on the shores of the New World. As the plantation culture began to thrive in Maryland and Virginia, small villages began to appear along the tidewater landscape. On Passerdyke Creek, a little place called Upper Trappe came into existence when landowners saw an opportunity to plant grains and corn along with tobacco. The waterway provided power for the grist mill, which could have been built as early as 1702. It was sold in 1763 to a local family, but remained an integral part of life in the village. Indentured servants toiled and often died in the difficult working conditions. That misery soon befell the newly imported African slaves. A divided plantation lifestyle was set into motion.

Still visible today, there are two properties remaining that predate the Revolutionary War. In 1665, Major Richard Bennett, a former governor of the colony of Virginia, received a large land patent. Bennett's Adventure, as it was called, was said to have been one of the largest on the Eastern Shore of Maryland at 2500 acres. In 1721, Colonel George Dashiell purchased the land and renamed it Dashiell's Lott. In 1733, he built a brick manor house there, which has survived to present time. The Dashiells would become one of the more prominent Eastern Shore family names, nearly synonymous with old money and social esteem. The other significant remaining property dates back to 1670, when James Dashiell had 500 acres of land along the Wicomico River. The land exchanged hands a few times until 1732 when Jonathan Bounds purchased it and built a residence there. The plantation was known as Bounds' Lott and the wooden framed house remains today.

With its white siding and green, slatted window shutters, three-story bell tower, and red brick walkways that lead up to carved wooden doors, the Asbury United Methodist Church, built in 1848, is picturesque and pastoral. Tucked in among weathered grave stones, shaded by cedar trees, and buffeted by farmland, it is simple in design and haunting in feel. In its earliest days, the church was heated by pot-bellied stoves and its members once started a Temperance movement. The sun has risen and set on this country church for decades, welcoming and enduring the changing seasons as generations of families have come and gone and come again.

Upper Trappe would become Allen around 1882, after the Civil War put an end to the plantation lifestyle. Tobacco and land grants from aristocrats fell out of favor while strawberries and small homesteads gained it. Stores and shops arose and modernity pushed the townspeople onward. Farmers and businessmen tended their duties while women raised their children — a new era upon them all. And the church was a mainstay for all those changes. Prior to the Civil War, slaves came to church with their owners, but sat in a gallery at the back; after the war, black church-goers attended nearby Friendship United Church. The segregation of blacks and whites in Allen mirrored every other town in rural Maryland. The social and cultural rules were understood by the division of its peoples and classes, the division of properties and places, the division of labor between men, and the expectations of women.

All of these historical notes reveal one truth: this is the kind of place in which the entire timeline of America can be seen and touched. Bennett's Adventure and Bounds' Lott, as well as the old Methodist church, are on the National Register of Historic Places. The grander homes of Allen's plantation era are now well-preserved relics, reminders of a bygone age. Other historic buildings were abandoned and lost, even the grist mill was torn down in 1919 to make way for better roads and a bridge. The long view of Allen is the short view of this country.

Not far from the church is the Allen Post Office. It closely resembles an early 20th century filling station and for good reason — it once was. The gas pumps are gone now. Also long vanished are the shops and stores from the turn of the previous century. Today, Allen is a bedroom community for the larger city of Salisbury. Modern conveniences are within reasonable driving distance, making a general store or butcher shop unnecessary now. Its mutations have taken centuries: from the colonial days of plantation living to the post-Civil War culture shifts to the emergence of industrial farming and planned neighborhoods with homes covered in vinyl siding.

Allen is a village of subtle transformations.

Across the street from the post office are several houses with paved driveways. One of these is a brick rancher with white shutters and a narrow front yard. It was once home to the Parsons family, well-known and respected in the community. Casey Parsons held a secure job with the state; Mary Belle Parsons was a busy homemaker. They married in October 1947, two years after the end of World War II. Their girls — Ellen, Barrie, and Alice — were bright, lovely, and polite. In that brick rancher on Allen Road, Casey and Mary Belle raised their three daughters, saw them married, met their grandchildren, and slipped into their silver years. When the time came, they were buried next to each other in the cemetery outside the gabled Asbury Methodist church.

For the Parsons family, Allen might as well have been Mayberry, an idyllic, safe place to raise a family where apple pies cooled on kitchen window sills and where one might spy a new Chevrolet in the neighbor's driveway. It was the kind of town where back doors were left unlocked and the minister was a shepherd to his flock, where people waved to folks driving by because rural Americans pride themselves on their friendly, down-home nature. Allen was and remains a place where time changes little and people can count on that sense of regularity.

But even in the smallest of communities where people can feel the most safe, despite that sense of familiarity and stability, bad things happen. Because sometimes the things to be afraid of are already home.

•   •   •   •   •

Mary Belle and Her Girls

The canon of stories within the Parsons family reflects warmth, humor, and a dichotomy between the parents. Often Casey plays the role of the mild-mannered, soft-hearted paternal figure while Mary Belle takes center stage for her larger-than-life personality, pithy wit, and commanding gaze. Her tongue was quick and sharp. If one of her girls came home, for example, suffering from some slight from another girl at school, Mary Belle's frequent response was simple: "Well, shit on them!" She displayed very little patience for anyone who did not rise to good social standards and if anyone were to question her children, well, God help them. In the little brick rancher on Allen Road, there was no question about who ruled.

She ran her household as a captain runs his ship. Because cleanliness was next to godliness in her eyes, the house was immaculate. Unexpected company arrived to a home perpetually ready for them: long white drapes, wingback chairs, Oriental rugs, wood surfaces that shone with the love and protection of elbow grease and Old English, and perhaps even gumdrops or butter mints in a cut crystal dish. Her meals were delicious and prepared with flourish. By lunchtime, she had already planned out their dinner, having run every errand in the morning, ready for her family by late afternoon. In the evenings, she and Casey often enjoyed a cocktail together as they relaxed in their perfect, suburban home. Proper and polite.

•   •   •   •   •

Mary Belle Smith had married her first husband and child-hood sweetheart, Robert Roscoe Malone, in June of 1940. She was 19 years old. The couple moved into an apartment in Salisbury where Mary Belle found work as a secretary for a packing company while Roscoe worked with the Eastern Shore Public Service Company, which provided electricity to local residents.

When the United States entered World War II, the young couple moved to a base in Quantico, Virginia where Roscoe began officer's training in the United States Marine Corps. As a lieutenant, Roscoe's orders took him to the Pacific, but it was to be a short-lived duty. In the spring of 1945, he was one of the more than 12,000 soldiers killed on Okinawa as the war reduced that tropical paradise to wet ashes. Roscoe was one of four men from Allen to die in the war. When the news reached the home front, Mary Belle became not only a widow but also a single mother. She had given birth to their daughter, Ellen, just six months prior, on November 24th, 1944.

Life for Mary Belle meant returning home to Allen. For a young single mother during the war, going back was the best way forward: she'd have family and friends to help her and offer support in the way that small communities so often do. Creating a new life in the close-knit familiarity of Allen was the surest and safest option. So in August 1945, she and little Ellen along with Mary Belle's cousin, Frances Anne, moved into a small summer cottage owned by Mary Belle's parents, a little property nicknamed "The Dollhouse." Frances had a three-year-old son and was recently divorced. There were lots of men coming home from the war and every weekend there were impromptu parties throughout the small towns of the Delmarva Peninsula. There were March of Dimes dances in the Salisbury armory where servicemen, crisp in their uniforms, met up with the local girls, flirting and laughing while they danced and drank into the early morning hours. It was a time of relief and elation. And love.

Frances wanted to go to the parties; Mary Belle was nervous and concerned because her in-laws lived just up the road. The Malones had lost their young son. *Might they find her attendance at these parties improper? What would people in town say about her? What would they think?* Mary Belle was a young woman in a little village with a small child. A lady's reputation was, for better or for worse, a commodity, and Mary Belle understood two things: societal rules mattered and good graces were essential.

Undeterred, Frances eventually coaxed her out of the house. One night in October 1946, at one of these impromptu post-war romps, Mary Belle was cornered in a closet by a chief petty officer. He had badgered and annoyed her so much she told Frances she would never even look at another officer. (Later in her life, Mary Belle would often say to her girls: "Never say never.") And yet, not even twenty four hours after her pledge, Mary Belle attended another party and made the acquaintance of another officer, Clarence "Casey" Louis Parsons from Pittsville, Maryland.

A year later, in October 1947, they were married.

• • • • •

During the early years of their marriage, Casey owned a small service station in his hometown of Pittsville, but Mary Belle, a stay-at-home mother to Ellen, began to demand more regular hours and wages. So, Casey obliged. He sold the gas station and accepted a position with the Maryland State Road Commission as a project engineer. Two more children arrived for Mary Belle and Casey Parsons: Barrie Ann on September 24th, 1950 and Alice Elizabeth on December 18th, 1955.

Ellen, the oldest, was beautiful, modest, and proper. Mary Belle and Ellen were close, and perhaps the loss of Roscoe, to whom Ellen bore a great resemblance, forged a special bond between them. Although Casey was her stepfather, she never called him anything but "dad" because he was the only father she had ever known. Ellen felt lucky because he treated her exactly as though she were his own child. Ellen grew up happy and contented and blossomed into a lovely young woman whose talents with a needle and thread were remarkable: she made Barrie's graduation dress by hand.

Barrie was the middle child, full of backbone and personality, with an aptitude for academics. She was a chatterbox, too. Mary Belle once lamented, "Barrie, you've got more mouth than a young crow!" From the beginning it was clear that Barrie was equal parts student, standout, and boss-in-training and it surprised no one in the family when, many years later, she became the first woman to be elected as mayor of Salisbury — a position she held for nearly a decade.

And then there was Alice, the baby of the family and named after Mary Belle's mother. She was a shy and quiet child, often displaying hints of her mother's quick cleverness. Alice was a bit on the pudgy side and needed glasses. In the fashion of the late 1950s, she wore a pair of cat-eye frames, the kind that pinched upward toward the temples, constantly giving a look of surprise or skepticism. Even as a small child, she looked like a seasoned librarian.

Mary Belle loved her girls. She was proud of their accomplishments and presentation within the community. She had lost

Roscoe, the one with whom she thought she'd make a life, but in Casey there was a second chance for everything — the model family, the perfect home, holidays and family gatherings, Sunday mornings at the old Methodist church, and quiet evenings at rest with a cocktail in hand, an entire world of their own making. They were friendly with other young couples in Allen for social events and outings, enjoying the camaraderie and friendship of other married folks with children the same age. Being a part of their community was important to the Parsons, and they were an ideal example of the post-war dream. And there in the center of everything, conducting the family's mood and movements, was Mary Belle. From any outsider's point of view, everything and everyone within the Parsons household was exactly as it should be.

But on the inside, Mary Belle knew better than to think she could control everything, and with three girls, she chose her battles. Ellen and Barrie, as sisters are known to do, fought endlessly. Anything and everything gave them cause to clash. Once, when Mary Belle tasked her two oldest daughters with washing and drying the dishes, there was an unforgettable row. While Ellen washed, Barrie snatched up a spoon and began to use it a makeshift microphone. She sang into the spoon and danced around the kitchen, doing a variety of things except drying the dishes. The dish rack filled up and soon Ellen ran out of patience. She reached up to grab the fly swatter from the top of the refrigerator to threaten her sister into proper submission and just as she did, she knocked over an entire container of gravy Mary Belle had left on top to cool. The gravy poured down Barrie's head and into the back of her shirt. As Ellen tells it, they both got into trouble; as Barrie tells it, Ellen got away scot-free.

Barrie bickered with Alice too. Perhaps it was just natural

friction caused by sharing close quarters, but even breathing posed a problem. When Alice was three, she broke her nose by smacking into a parked car while riding her tricycle in the front yard. The result was a chronic and terrible snore. At night, Barrie gritted her teeth at the very sound of Alice's rumbling inhalations.

Ellen, however, saw Alice in a different sisterly light. She was eleven years old (and Barrie was just five) when Alice was born so the prospect of a newborn baby meant having a real life baby doll. Ellen took to Alice immediately, changing her diapers and dressing her up in different outfits. Whatever frustrations the middle sister had with the baby of the family — and perhaps it was the age difference — Ellen had none. She took on a secondary mother role, loving and doting on their happy little sister.

Alice seemed content when she was alone. Mary Belle once forgot to pick up Alice from first grade. Upon realizing her mistake, she hopped in her car, a 1961 Ford, and headed toward Fruitland Primary School. She saw a little girl walking along the side of the road, lunch box and school bag in hand, near the Circle Bar on Camden Avenue. *I think that looks like Alice*, she said to herself and whipped the car around. Sure enough, it was. Realizing she'd been forgotten, six-year-old Alice struck off and headed home, and had made it more than a mile on her own. No tears, no great upset, just simple resolve.

That was how Alice fit into the family. Unassuming. Moving about in her own quiet way. No quarreling. No instigation. When Ellen invited her boyfriend over, Barrie would spy on her or sneak into her room. Barrie pushed her buttons and Ellen retaliated. Such is the give and take of sisterhood. But when it was Alice's turn to spy on Barrie and her beaus on the sofa or to sneak into Barrie's private things, she wouldn't do it. No matter how much Barrie provoked her, Alice would never reciprocate for sisterly indiscretions. Alice never fought back or tried to get even. There was no resistance.

Alice would not take her pound of flesh from anyone.

• • • • •

"It's gonna be alright."

Gale Glasgow burst into hot, quick tears as she and half of her first grade class entered a new classroom. A sea of new faces stared back at her. *What was happening? And why?* On the first day of school, she had been assigned to a teacher she really liked and now, for some reason unknown to her, the class had been divided. Her half was sent away from the comfortable room and teacher she knew. Gale was devastated by the change, and as she surveyed the new room, the new teacher, and the other kids, her tears began to flow.

Just then, a little girl with cat-eye glasses walked over and put her arms around Gale's shoulders.

"Don't cry. It's gonna be alright," she said.

The gentle touch was a great comfort and Gale calmed down. Wiping the tears from her face, she looked at the young girl with the cat-eye glasses. Her face was kind and her expression friendly. She had chestnut brown hair with straight, short bangs. Her glasses sat on round cheeks, one with an obvious dimple, and magnified a pair of bright blue eyes. The little girl wore a crisp dress with a pattern of tiny flowers, ruffled at the cap sleeves, and a white Peter Pan collar. In the space of a few seconds, Gale no longer felt alone or afraid. This little girl was standing by her, easing her worries. From that moment forward, Gale Glasgow and Alice Parsons were best friends.

Gale Glasgow was the proverbial country mouse, born and raised on the Glasgow family farm on Glasgow Road on the outskirts of Salisbury. She came from a family of truck farmers who raised crops and sold them at local auctions. It was a long-standing rural occupation, dating back decades on the Delmarva Peninsula. Entire families, from grandparents down to grandchildren, worked the fields of homestead farms. Each season called for different crops to plant, nuture, harvest, package, deliver, and sell. Beyond the crops, there were ceaseless chores, like tending livestock, canning food, and fixing machinery. The work on a family farm was back-breaking and rarely lucrative, and it created generations of tough people who proudly embraced a culture of resiliency and self-reliance. This is the kind of life Gale knew.

Alice and her family lived a middle-class and professional life just a few miles away in Allen proper. The first time Gale went to visit Alice, Gale was seven years old and was dumbstruck by the trip. The streets were so crowded and the yards were so little! She had never seen that many houses on one street so close together. Alice lived in a red brick house with a manicured lawn. Once inside, Gale marveled at the beautiful furniture. In front of the sofa, there was a polished butler's table with shiny hinges. A pretty brass box sat on top. The dining room table had beautiful china already set out like a fancy dinner might happen at any second. Gale began to understand that Alice's life in this wonder of a home was nothing like her life on the farm.

The two girls may have come from sharply contrasting places, but that mattered little to them. They liked each other. Alice was kind to Gale and Gale was loyal to Alice. Childhood friendships are just that simple. Whether they were playing games or trudging through the woods or wandering around Allen with their pockets full of candy, the girls were inseparable. Alice and Gale; Gale and Alice. Best friends, side by side, no matter what.

•   •   •   •   •

Not long after their friendship began, one day in school, Gale witnessed something strange, something she had never seen before. She looked over at her new friend, but Alice wasn't looking back. She wasn't looking anywhere at all. It was like she was staring off into the distance. Then, her eyes began to roll backward and Alice's head slipped to the side. The pencil in her hand fell to the floor. Before Gale could raise her hand or call out or jump to her feet, Alice dropped to the floor.

The teacher rushed to Alice's side. Gale too. By the time they reached her, Alice was coming to. The other students stared at Alice. For a few hushed moments, the classroom was stilled as Alice regained her full consciousness. Gale was scared at first, but that soon gave way to concern. In the episode, Alice had wet herself. The teacher arranged for Mary Belle to bring fresh clothes to school and the lesson continued. But Gale would never forget this moment because it was the first of many more to come.

Alice was born with a mild form of childhood epilepsy. Her family and others referred to these episodes as "spells," a common term at the time. Today, doctors refer to it as childhood absence epilepsy, and it happens to otherwise healthy children who typically outgrow the condition around puberty without any permanent effects. There is no brain damage associated with the condition. Unlike a typical "grand mal" seizure of full body convulsions, these types of "petit mal" seizures are more benign. In Alice's case, her head would fall back, her eyes would roll or go blank, her face would be void of emotion or expression with her mouth frozen or drooped, and she wouldn't be able to speak or hear. It was as if she suddenly wasn't there, as though she were staring off into space. If she was holding something in her hands, it would fall to the floor. These seizures happened several times a day and each lasted a few seconds, but in those brief moments, Alice was lost.

The epilepsy quickly formed a barrier between Alice and her peers. She seemed to sense she was different from the other kids. Often Alice would awake and find people standing over her or huddled around her, staring at her, but she wouldn't remember what had happened. Gale stood by her side during many of these episodes, often picking up her dropped books or pencils and reassuring her once Alice had regained herself, but it was awkward and embarrassing for a young girl. Alice, already a shy child, began to turn inward.

And Gale was there to watch Alice begin to build her walls.

• • • • •

The Wing and The Sparrow

Alice's epilepsy worried Mary Belle and terrified Casey; they never knew when a seizure would occur and what might happen to Alice when it did. With little advanced medicine on the lower Eastern Shore, they struggled to find help. In the late 1950s and early 1960s, seeking medical attention was difficult for rural parents. The University of Maryland sent a specialist once a month from Baltimore to see a large number of patients on the Eastern Shore, but because Alice's seizures were not convulsive or prolonged, she was bumped down the list.

It was maddening. Casey's worry continued to mount, and he became increasingly overprotective as he watched his youngest daughter struggle daily with seizures. He committed himself to keeping a watchful eye over her. If Alice wanted to ride her bike, Casey would run along beside her, fearful that she might have a seizure while riding; if he wasn't home, then she'd have to wait until he returned. *What if she were riding her bike and had a seizure and got hurt without anyone around to help her?* No, Alice wasn't allowed to take risks. He could not bear the thought of her being hurt. He had to protect her.

By the time she reached the fourth grade, Mary Belle and Casey were frustrated and desperate for help. One doctor prescribed a drug that turned Alice into a child zombie. She was overmedicated and barely hanging on in school, unable to stay awake. At night, Mary Belle and Barrie would finish Alice's homework for her so she wouldn't fall behind in school.

Casey felt helpless. He could do nothing for his little girl except watch her head fall back, eyes go blank, and slip away. He winced at knowing Alice would often wake up to see her classmates staring at her, especially if it resulted in a bladder accident. It broke his heart to think of the embarassment she must have felt but kept locked inside. So he provided sanctuary for her: she was his wounded sparrow and he kept her safe by keeping her close, under his shielding wing. It was all he knew to do.

• • • • •

Casey Parsons had enlisted in the Navy in August 1939. He was serving aboard the Destroyer *USS Russell* in the North Atlantic when Pearl Harbor was attacked on December 7, 1941. They received orders to head to the Pacific immediately. As the *USS Russell* passed by New York City without its running lights, Casey saw a great metropolis under a total blackout. No lights, no movement, nothing. It was only four days into the war and he was struck by the all-encompassing darkness. The haunting scene, like the end of the world as he knew it, stayed with him. He knew he would be facing something awful, something he couldn't quite imagine yet. They passed through the Panama Canal on New Year's Day in 1942 and arrived in Pearl Harbor later that month. There, Casey saw the unimaginable. Graves dug along the white sandy beach. Twisted hulks of metal. The wreckage of planes and ships motionless beneath the crystal blue waters. And the awful toll: 2400 Americans dead and 1200 more injured. Agony and anger. Hawaii was revered in the States for being beautiful and exotic, a colonized Eden for honeymooners, and now the men saw it blackened by fires and scarred by the ravages of war. Those men would never erase those images from their minds.

Casey saw war up close when, in June 1942, the *Russell* was involved in the Battle of Midway, often called the "turning point of the Pacific War." The Japanese hoped to strike a massive blow to the United States and Allies, but when U.S. forces, including the *Russell*, sank four of Japan's aircraft carriers, the notion of an American defeat evaporated on the horizon. During the Battle of Midway, the men aboard the *Russell* witnessed an awful event: Japanese fighter planes delivered a series of fatal blows to the *USS Yorktown*, causing its abandonment and eventual capsizing. They watched as it faltered and sank beneath the waves.

Casey Parsons, then 22, was from the serene farm fields and backwoods of the rural Eastern Shore of Maryland. He was far from home and the familiar waters of the Chesapeake and the Atlantic, miles and miles away from the cornfields and the forested landscapes of his youth. Childhood memories of playing in a canoe seemed like a lifetime ago as he found himself homesick in the belly of an iron warship in the unfamiliar and dangerous waters of the South Pacific. War was real; men were dying; and no one knew what lay beyond the horizon anymore. In his twilight years, he once wrote: "Sometimes, between the flashes of gunfire, I could see more clearly than before, the hitching post by the general store and the old shell road."

Over the next two years, the men of the *Russell* found themselves all over the Pacific Ocean: Guadalcanal, Australia, Kiska Island, Mare Island, New Zealand, and the Marshall Islands. The *Russell* earned 16 battle stars, making it among the most decorated ships in World War II. Sometime in 1944, Casey transferred to the *USS Frank Knox*. He was aboard that ship on September 2nd, 1945 in the Tokyo Bay when the news broke: the Japanese had surrendered. At long last, the war was over, and in November, Casey Parsons ended his military career as a chief fire control officer and headed home. He had survived the war and now had his entire life ahead of him. He would raise a family in a world and in a country he had helped make possible. Evil vanquished; enemies subjugated. This is what he fought for: freedom and safety.

• • • • •

For the girls, especially Alice, there was refuge in Casey. He was the easy touch to their mother's disciplinarian disposition. He loved words and reading, possibly living with a regret that he should have gone to college after the war. Might he have been an English professor or a history teacher? Casey scribbled passages of Shakespeare within the pages of his State Highway Administration manual so he could read them during breaks. He read them to Alice who later developed a deep fondness for the English playwright. He also enjoyed reading history, especially naval history; in the evenings, the girls could find Casey reading biographies of Winston Churchill and the like. (During the American Bi-Cenntenial in 1976, Alice bore the American flag in the Allen parade, a moment that no doubt caused his heart to swell with fatherly and patriotic pride.)

When Alice was twelve years old, Casey — still refusing to give up — found another doctor, this time at Johns Hopkins, who helped get her seizures under control. By this time, her condition was reaching its natural end as she moved towards puberty and the seizures became less frequent. However, Casey's overprotective nature didn't decline proportionately. Alice would remain under his wing as he sheltered her from storms, both real and imagined.

•   •   •   •   •

American Pie and Cheap Beer

By the early 1970s, Casey and Mary Belle had a quieter house with only one bird left in their nest. Ellen, who was working at a local library, had married Scott Hitch and they were raising their daughter, Kim. In a switching of roles, Alice took to Kim just as Ellen had taken to Alice when she was little. Barrie, who was enrolled at Hood College, soon followed her older sister's lead when she married Mat Tilghman. Gone were the days of screaming sisters and spying on boyfriends. Alice missed Barrie terribly and spoke of her often. Gale only had brothers at home and had always wanted a sister so she lived vicariously through Alice's tales of Ellen and Barrie.

As Gale and Alice moved through their school years, one social rule became increasingly apparent to them: they were not going to be part of the popular crowd. Within the halls of James M. Bennett Junior and Senior High Schools, it seemed the cool kids would have no use for a country bumpkin like Gale or a shy, four-eyed girl like Alice. They had entered the material age of having the right clothes and accessories; a quick look revealed who was shopping at Salisbury's well-heeled stores like Benjamin's and Hess Apparel, and who was relegated to Sears. It felt like a rigged game they could never win, but even so, Gale sometimes wondered, what if they did dress like they had just waltzed out of Hess Apparel? Then could they be part of the high school aristocracy? But Gale and Alice knew better.

Outside of school, it was often just the two of them. Together, they spent their nights curled up on a sofa watching *The Mary Tyler Moore Show* or holed up in one of their bedrooms with a copy of the latest yearbook, and making fun of all the popular kids or as they called them, "the clique kids." Alice mimicked their voices as they gave them nicknames and recited their flaws. The girls laughed and giggled as the Beatles and Carole King sang in the background. This was their secret revenge on the kids who excluded them. It wasn't that the other kids picked on them. It was that the other kids never even saw them. They might as well have been invisible. Gale and Alice even sneaked into the Class of '72 graduation exercises solely for the purpose of making fun of "the clique kids."

Alice and Gale loved Don McLean's "American Pie" and it became their anthem of sorts. Gale suggested they tie-dye their jeans and wear pink carnations on their blue chambray work shirts. And they did. They paraded down the halls of Bennett Senior High School, waiting for someone to ask them about their outfits, but no one did. No one noticed. That was fine by Alice, though, because those pink carnations meant something to her. It meant having a best friend, someone with whom she could share inside jokes and secrets. It meant she *belonged*.

The two girls shared everything, including their deepest-held fears and worries. Alice spoke of how Mary Belle could be harsh at times even under the watchful eye of Casey. Gale listened as Alice recounted a few heated arguments she had with Mary Belle whose strong and forceful nature often ran counter to Alice's introspective personality. Gale always felt sorry for Alice, especially after one particularly awful battle. Maybe it was just a mother's exasperation with a teenage daughter. Maybe Mary Belle was angry about something else and Alice was on the receiving end of her tongue. Maybe Alice was being stubborn or self-possessed as she had a tendency to be. Either way, when Alice got to school, she told her best friend about the terrible fight. Gale felt heartbroken for her, but she noticed Alice was perfectly stoic about it. She wasn't crying or acting out. She just repeated the words as though they were part of a book report. Gale could barely understand it all. Alice just took it in. Kept it beneath the surface, pushed way down into another part of her.

While Alice confided in her best friend, Gale returned in kind, admitting that her father was an alcoholic. His addiction was a hardship, and given that her family wasn't affluent like the Parsons, times could get rough on the farm. Once, while Alice was spending the night with Gale, the heat went off in the house during a cold winter evening. The two girls hunkered down under a mass of blankets in Gale's bed while Cat Stevens crooned "Wild World" on the radio.

During the school year, it was easy for the girls to stay close, but that came to a halt during the summer. Those months, Gale and Alice had to work. Alice got a job at the same library as Ellen while Gale rolled up her sleeves on the farm and sorted watermelons into giant piles and hauled bushels of corn onto pickups and trailers. In a way, their summer jobs were reflections of their lives: Alice surrounded by books while Gale had her hands in the dirt.

Within their respective families, the girls felt like outsiders, as teenage girls often do. Perhaps as an act of rebellion, the girls drank. They stole Cabin Still bourbon whiskey from Casey and Mary Belle's liquor cabinet, which always was well-stocked. One night, an ex-boyfriend gave Gale a six-pack of cheap Lowenbrau beer. Because Gale's father was an alcoholic, they had to be sneaky lest they get caught by her mother who had long put her foot down about having alcohol in her house. Gale's father had taken to hiding bottles in the bushes and trees. The girls smuggled the package, disguised as a gift, into the house and hid it inside a box in the vegetable drawer of the refrigerator. They spent the night sneaking down to the kitchen and trying not to get caught by Gale's mother. These were carefully concealed moments, a harmless rite of passage for two high school girls on the outside, always looking in. Whenever Gale overdid it, Alice was there to take care of her. But the roles never reversed. Despite drinking right alongside Gale, Alice never lost control, never let go.

The girls didn't always have to drink in secret, though. The legal drinking age in Maryland in the 1970s was 18. Even in the Parsons home, the notion of two 17-year-old girls drinking wasn't overly offensive. Drinking was a normal social activity, a rite of passage. Alice had her first martini at 15. In one instance, Casey made a pitcher of Bloody Marys and announced the first one to finish would get the last glass. Gale won that challenge.

Just before the start of their senior year, Gale caught the eye of Dean Dashiell, a nice young man from a good family. For the Eastern Shore, the Dashiells were blue bloods, and by the time Gale and Dean started dating, the family name was tied to the most prominent builders. Gale was happy in her newfound love, and she wanted the same thing for Alice. Wouldn't it be nice if they could go on double dates? The problem was twofold: Alice was painfully shy and boys were not showing any interest. Gale constantly tried to nudge Alice to talk to a friend of Dean's, but Alice couldn't or wouldn't build up the nerve to talk to him no matter how much Gale prodded.

As their prom approached, Gale renewed her efforts and outright begged her to call Dean's friend, but again she was met with resistance. Nothing could move Alice and so Gale decided she wouldn't go either. They had stuck together through thick and thin from first grade to their senior year, and as they stared down the final months of school, prom began to look like just another moment of teenage glory for the cool kids.

Until it wasn't.

When Dean's mother found out, she pleaded with Gale to reconsider and take her son to prom. Dean had missed his prom and she wanted more than anything to see him dressed up and headed off to the big dance like other teenage boys. His mother said she'd even buy Gale's dress, which had been her last remaining holdout. Softened by these appeals, Gale reluctantly accepted and trudged off to purchase a gown from Hess Apparel. Just as her classmates were getting excited, in equal measure, Gale was filling with dread. She didn't want to go without her best friend.

The seniors chose a futuristic "2001" as the theme for their big dance, complete with stars and moons and even a big rocket ship. On the eve of prom, Gale was near tears. No one had asked Alice and, for her part, Alice hadn't made an issue of it, but Gale felt guilty for having a boyfriend and for going to the dance without Alice. It didn't feel right to be there without her best friend. She stared at her gown and its puffy sleeves, and she wished she were staying home.

Gale had watched as Alice routinely shut out boys and balked at the very notion of a boyfriend. She seemed settled to be without a romantic interest and without ever having gone on a date with a boy. As far as Gale knew, Alice had never even been kissed. Yet Gale was sure Alice must have wanted something more. Doesn't every girl long for first love? For that moment when boy meets girl and suddenly the world is revealed in a new light? Holding hands and red roses, stolen kisses and warm embraces: Gale felt this way with Dean. It was love and it was sweet and wonderful. After all, Gale and Alice were young women on the cusp of womanhood. Wasn't that what all those singers were talking about in those songs they listened to? Record after record about falling in love and being together, the faithful leaping of a heart ready and willing to see what lies ahead?

Didn't Alice want any of those things?

That night, while the James M. Bennett Class of 1973 danced in the gym and laughed and sang under cut-out stars as the music played on, Gale thought about their lives. Dean would likely propose one day and she'd accept. He was everything she wanted and Gale felt certain he was the one for her. And then there was Alice, her best friend since first grade. Gale loved Alice and cherished their times together. From that first moment of standing by her side in a new classroom to spilling her deepest secrets to every song they had sung together sitting on the floor of Alice's bedroom, every moment of their long friendship meant the world to Gale. Things were going to change now. She knew Alice was headed off to college in Towson. But beyond that point, Gale couldn't see anything. Alice's life appeared as a mystery as she remained reserved and guarded. Gale wondered what would happen to her in college. Would Alice ever let a man get close to her?

• • • • •

The Long Way Home

Gale stayed in Salisbury and continued to date Dean while Alice went off to Towson University to get her degree in English, perhaps just as Casey might have wished for himself. Gale and Alice wrote letters and spent time with each other when Alice came home for the holidays. Once, Gale and Dean drove to Alice's dorm in Towson. Leslie Hickok, Alice's cousin, was there and they drove into Washington, D.C. for an Elton John concert. Gale wore a pair of navy blue Mary Jane shoes with a platform, and Alice took one look at her feet and wisecracked, "Are you going to do a tap dance routine tonight?" They burst into laughter, and in that moment, Gale had a glimpse of her old high school friend, the one who made fun of the cool kids and impersonated their voices, the one who always seemed to size up the world around her in a flash. She wanted to hold onto her friendship with Alice, hoping that they could remain close despite the changes in their worlds, but it wasn't to be. The frequency of their letters began to dwindle over Alice's four years at Towson. Gale accepted that Alice was busy and had new friends. Their friendship began to diminish with time and distance and separate life experiences.

Alice graduated in 1977 and took a job in Washington, D.C. with a lobbyist organization for groups like Avon and Mary Kay. She liked her roommate, Rosemary, and she even liked her boss, Eileen. In later years, Alice would often quote her: "It doesn't get done by talking about it." Eileen was a take-charge kind of woman, reminiscent of Mary Belle. Alice tried to make a go of it, but try as she might, the fast-paced lifestyle of the big city didn't agree with her.

Dating had also proved unfulfilling. Alice dated an Iranian man for a time, but the relationship fizzled out. No one knew much about him, but for her family and friends, there was concern because American and Iranian tensions were high. The 1979-1981 hostage crisis created distrust and a sense of being wary of the enemy. Gale knew of another woman who married an Iranian man and had children with him. He moved the entire family back to Iran, and Gale had heard he threatened their children whenever she made any mention of wanting to return to the United States. This made Gale worry. Alice's sisters also held similar reservations. Coming from such diametrically opposed backgrounds, how would Alice and the Iranian man work out? Would he want her to move to the Middle East? Would she be safe with him? The relationship set her family and friends on edge, and everyone was relieved when Alice indicated the relationship was over.

After a year and a half in D.C., Alice briefly moved in with Barrie and Mat who were living in Easton, Pennsylvania. They had a young son, Andrew. It was a happy time between the sisters. Barrie had outgrown her childhood frustrations with her little sister, and Alice held no grudges. They were grown women now, making kinder memories with one another. In the evenings, they sat on the sofa with their feet kicked up, side by side, eating pickles as they watched *Poldark* on PBS. Alice played with her nephew, smiling down at him while bouncing him on her knee. She loved being an aunt to Kim and now Andrew. But Pennsylvania still wasn't home and so Alice returned to the little brick rancher in Allen with Mary Belle and Casey, right back where she started.

• • • • •

"Love looks not with the eyes, but with the mind."

Back home in Allen, she was once again under the protective gaze of Mary Belle and Casey, but this time, she wasn't a chubby little girl with glasses and epilepsy. Alice, about 24 years old, was now an attractive young woman with soft features: her chestnut brown hair brushed the tops of her shoulders, feathered back in a style reminiscent of Farah Fawcett. Her blue eyes no longer hid behind glasses, and when she smiled, her cherubic cheeks became even more pronounced. She was tall, just about 5'8", and she carried herself like a lady. Although there were no suitors knocking on the front door of the Parsons home, Alice gave no indication that was a problem. Alice seemed content to be without a romantic interest. Instead, she focused on what she would do for a career; she had to establish herself in the world, especially given that she was unreliant on a husband of her own. What did she want to do?

When she had been a little girl, she used to play school. Her students were imaginary, which her sisters found amusing, but the experience, even in a silly charade, put Alice in control. She could be the one to make the rules and take command. She already had a head-start from her four years at Towson, and she soon announced to her family that she planned to enroll at Salisbury State College to get her degree in Elementary Education.

Alice Parsons was going to become an English teacher.

Her family happily received the news. Ellen thought back to their childhood, recalling how Alice — all alone in her make-believe world — taught the lessons and carried on as if her pupils were rapt with attention. For Ellen, it was a tender sight to behold.

Barrie found it a little strange because she could never recall a moment in which grown-up Alice said she wanted to be a teacher. And more to the point, as shy as Alice was, could she manage a bunch of unruly kids? But the Parsons family loved Alice and they wholeheartedly supported her decision. Maybe it was a decision written in the stars: Alice's namesake, her maternal grandmother Alice Higgins Smith Messick, once served as a teacher at the Allen school in 1902.

In the meanwhile, Alice took an office job at the Price Buick car dealership on Route 13 in Salisbury. There, one of her co-workers decided to set Alice up on a blind date with one of the used car salesmen. His name was Jess Henry Davis. It would be a double date; the foursome would meet at the bar in the Sheraton Hotel in downtown Salisbury. It was Memorial Day weekend, 1980. Alice was nervous, but she steeled her resolve with a few drinks and waited. The minutes ticked by, but Jess never came. Adding insult to injury, Alice fainted in the bathroom of the hotel bar and had to be taken to the emergency room. Maybe she hadn't eaten enough. Maybe even a couple of drinks were too much. Maybe her nerves got the best of her. Perhaps it was a combination of all those things, but it had all the hallmarks of those childhood days when her epilepsy made her feel abnormal. The blind date had been a disaster and it embarrassed Alice so much that she asked Ellen's husband, Scott, who worked at the hospital, to intercept the ER bill so that her parents would not see it in the mail. Although her sisters knew, Alice kept that night a secret from Mary Belle and Casey.

With that, the Parsons girls wrote off Jess Davis and bid him good riddance.

• • • • •

Jess Henry Davis, Jr. was born on December 30th, 1953 to Doris Dougherty and Jess Henry Davis, Sr. near Egg Harbor, New Jersey. He was the youngest of two children, with an older sister named Patricia. His mother, Doris, was the youngest of seven children. Her parents, James and Catherine Dougherty, started their family in Somerset County, Maryland and then moved to Atlantic County, New Jersey. That's where they lived when Doris was born and it's where Jess grew up in less-than-idyllic circumstances.

Jess's biological father was an alcoholic who ran around on his wife. His stepfather was a stern man who had served in the Navy. There is a family story that he might have been a SEAL. He was physically, verbally, and emotionally abusive to Doris's children. Jess, later in his life, told a story about how one time his stepfather erupted at him during dinner, yelling at him, "You want to eat like a pig, then eat like a pig!" Jess said his stepfather slammed his head into a plate full of food on the floor and made him eat it on all fours like a pig at a trough. Like a mongrel dog. But for all the abuse he took at the hands of his stepfather, Jess maintained an outward, happy-go-lucky attitude and was known for being a helpful guy. During one cold New Jersey winter, he literally took the coat off his back and gave it to a friend who didn't have one. He was that kind of kid, who, despite coming from hard circumstances, appeared determined to lend a hand, and if all else failed, at least make them laugh.

The home was fraught with agitation and cruelty, which resulted in Jess moving out as a teenager. He bounced around, going to live with various nearby relatives from time to time. During one of these moves while he was living with an aunt, one of Jess's friends introduced him to Nancy*, a young girl from his neighborhood.

---

* *Her name has been changed for privacy.*

Jess took her to her senior prom at Oakcrest High School.

They dated, got serious, and in 1977, Jess and Nancy had a daughter, Lori. The relationship was no fairytale as she began to realize Jess wasn't always the wise-cracking joker he appeared to be. Tension and anger seeped in. It wasn't the family life Nancy had hoped for and she began to see troubling signs emerging in Jess: secrecy, criminality, and duplicity. Once she found several small marijuana plants tucked behind their couch. She also discovered he was cheating on her with other women. There was a pattern forming. As he moved from boyhood into manhood, he was turning into an amalgamation of the iniquitous men in his life: like his biological father, Jess was a lady's man who lied and cheated without compunction, and like his stepfather, he could be a menacing bully.

One day in 1979, Nancy was in the car with Lori, getting ready to go run a few errands. Lori was standing on the front seat next to her. Out of the corner of her eye, Nancy saw Jess quickly approaching the driver's side of the car. He was screaming and before she could react, he had reached in through the open car window and yanked the keys from the ignition. Nancy pleaded with him, but Jess was enraged. Nancy realized she couldn't get away from him, not by car nor on foot. She felt trapped; he essentially held them hostage in the parking lot. The altercation was punctuated by little Lori's cries of "Give mommy keys!" Nancy had no idea how this fight would end, but just as suddenly as he had turned so hot, he cooled off. He handed her the keys and let her go.

Living in a home with Jess Davis was no place and no situation for raising a daughter. Nancy left him and took Lori with her. Jess moved permanently to Maryland, likely because of his family connections in Somerset County. Once he was gone, he rarely sent child support and he never went to see his daughter. Jess Davis, it seemed, was out of their lives for good, but even though he was gone, Nancy remained uneasy.

•   •   •   •   •

Despite the disastrous evening at the Sheraton, Alice decided to give Jess Davis a second chance, and that night changed everything for her. It was August of 1980. He took her to a nightclub called The Paddock in Ocean City, Maryland to see The Diamonds, a 1950s and 60s cover band. The Paddock was a prominent bar on the beach strip, established in the 1950s as an entertainment destination where, as local rumors have it, even Louis Armstrong once played. By the early 1980s, however, The Paddock had earned a wild reputation as an oceanside hotspot for loud music and drinking and dancing. The Chippendales, an all-male exotic dancing squad, once performed a strip tease on the small but well-lit stage. It was exactly the sort of place that inexperienced Alice Parsons didn't frequent. In the dimly lit atmosphere punctuated by flashes of colored disco lights and trapped by a low ceiling, Jess led her through a throng of sweaty, moving bodies. She could feel the vibrations moving through her, around her. Alice — the girl who had shied away from her own prom — was now dancing in a nightclub with a stranger, a man with ice blue eyes and the intensity of a small sun.

Her universe might as well have been upside down, and there was Jess at the center of it all. He sang nearly every word of every song and Alice thought it was funny, charming even. She considered this man in front of her, this stranger serenading her to the music of her childhood, and she became fascinated with him. He told her she was beautiful. He said he couldn't believe his luck in being set up with a woman like her. Oh, and her blue eyes were gorgeous, he remarked. When the subject of their first date came up, Jess explained that he had been fishing and the boat broke down and that was the reason he didn't show up. For Alice, it must have been an acceptable, logical explanation.

That night with Jess, something happened to Alice. The electricity of first passion and romantic thoughts about a man — *this man* — charged her. It was intoxicating for Alice. As they danced under the dazzling colored lights, she felt his body close to hers and her pulse raced. She could smell his cologne and it made her head swim. Feelings she had not yet known as a woman collided with the rawness of her inexperience; Alice, at 24, had never been with a man, but now she wanted to be. She wanted him. All those serious and secretive parts of her that she had guarded for so many years were now vulnerable as she suddenly found herself inexplicably and undeniably lovestruck. And then a single thought flashed in her mind: *this is the one. He is the one.*

The next morning, she called Barrie, gushing about how she had finally met him and how they connected and how she had never met anyone like him. Barrie was confused and irritated. Why had Alice given this guy another chance? This guy who ditched her on the first date and, by their account, caused her to end up in the hospital? But Alice insisted that it was a misunderstanding and everything was wonderful.

The more Barrie questioned her, the clearer the answer became: Alice had fallen in love.

•   •   •   •   •

"Nothing good can come of this."

The poor first impression the sisters had of Jess Davis did not improve upon meeting him. When Barrie finally met Jess, she saw a man who seemed to embody blandness, mediocrity. He wasn't tall or short, fat or thin, good-looking or ugly, strong or weak. He was basic and average in almost every physical way with the exception that, like Alice, he had remarkably blue eyes. In conversation he was awkward; in humor he was crass. Barrie could not understand what her college-educated and intelligent sister saw in him. Jess was a high school graduate who sold Buicks. He had a child in New Jersey from whom he was estranged, and Barrie's limited knowledge of that situation made her apprehensive. He seemed to be floating along with all the ambition, responsibility, and determination of a dandelion seed caught in a wandering breeze.

Ellen was cautious around Jess because she, like the rest of the family, just wanted Alice to be happy. But there was something about him that bothered her. There was a shadiness, a shifty quality to his braggadocious persona, like his repeated claims about finding a dead baby mouse in the bottom of a Coca-Cola bottle. He raised such a ruckus about it that the Parsons family began to wonder if he was trying to extort some entity for money over it. There was even a rumor circulating through their social circles that Coca-Cola had hired a local man who was a retired FBI agent to look into his claims and follow Jess around. Ellen never believed Jess, but kept her opinion of it to herself. She felt maybe he was looking for a quick payoff or hush money, but it troubled Ellen that Alice was involved with a man who would proclaim personal experience with what everyone knew to be an urban legend. It was just so ... odd.

Mary Belle found him unsuitable. He was a braggart, a real bullshitter. He hadn't served in the military nor had he gone to college. He had a child he was not raising or supporting, a moral point that undoubtedly put Jess in an unsavory light for a woman of convention like Mary Belle. "Nothing good can come of this," she told Barrie privately during the courtship. It was a reflection of her earnest worry that Jess would not be able to provide for Alice. She had seen it before: Casey's sister married an abusive and difficult man and so Mary Belle knew just how hard a life could be for a woman in that kind of circumstance. She didn't want any of that for Alice. She wanted more for her, which is as natural an inclination as a mother could have. Mary Belle was of the school that believed a woman should marry upward, or at a minimum, laterally. Jess Davis represented the worst direction — down. A life with Jess meant that Alice would never have the things a mother wishes for a daughter: comfort, security, and good social standing. Jess was shaping up to be the black sheep in the family.

When her family questioned her, arguments ensued. The comparison was hard to miss. Her sisters were accomplished in their professional lives and had married well to young men of good social standing. Scott Hitch would go onto become a well-liked hospital executive and Mat Tilghman, the owner of a successful insurance agency. Mary Belle approved of the pairings, especially since her oldest two daughters had started families of their own, giving Casey and Mary Belle grandchildren. Ellen and Scott had Kim and Barrie and Mat had Andrew and Catherine, who went by the nickname "Casey." The Hitch and Tilghman families were on respectable, solid paths. And then there was Jess, loud and crude and devoid of any sense of the professional aspirations or the social graces admired by Mary Belle. Jess was like a feral cat brought indoors for the first time: jumpy and ill at ease, always caterwauling about one thing or another, and in need of sustained supervision lest it ruin the rugs or damage the drapes.

No one seemed to understand the attraction. Except Alice.

She had fallen in love for the first time in her young life and deeply so. The potency of first love is a powerful thing, creating a bottomless pit of emotions, and Alice found herself unable to resist the untamable Jess Davis. There was something enrapturing about him. He was a heady combination of bad boy and wounded child. He had secrets and a rough upbringing which made him vulnerable, but he hid all that behind his masculinity and bravado. With Alice, he had let his guard down so that only she could see through the swagger and glimpse the complexity within him. Because of her empathetic nature, Alice *understood* him.

The older sisters gave up questioning and arguing with Alice because it only served to push her further away from them. They loved Alice and wanted only the best for her, yet there was a growing undertow in their relationships. Alice, as Barrie and Ellen saw it, was annoyed by their "snobbish" or unwelcoming attitude towards Jess, which only fueled her need to defend him and his meager and difficult background. Barrie and Ellen wanted common ground, but a rift was forming.

Mary Belle and Casey also began to sidestep the topic of Jess's suitability, a maneuver that became increasingly difficult as the couple grew more serious about one another. While they dated, Alice continued to live at home with her parents in Allen, even after she graduated from Salisbury State College in 1981 with a Bachelor's Degree in Elementary Education. Jess lived with a few of his buddies in a rented house not far from Alice's old high school in Salisbury. The neighborhood was often referred to as "the Princeton homes." The houses were small, generally prefabricated construction or remnants of the World War II housing boom, and they lined Princeton Avenue and its intersecting streets with common names like John, Roger, Margaret, and Cecil. It was considered a "starter home" neighborhood for young working-class couples, unlike the newer suburban neighborhoods of Rustic Acre, Deer Harbor, and Centennial Village where white collar folks lived on streets with names like Ramblin Road, Lost Fawn Drive, and Cobblestone Court. In the Princeton Homes neighborhood, Jess was living a carefree bachelor's life, working during the day and drinking in bars at night, while Alice was still sleeping in her childhood bedroom.

• • • • •

"If everyone would just do their job!"

With her new degree in hand, Alice started out by taking substitute teaching positions around the county. Someone from the hiring department at the Wicomico County Board of Education called to offer her a temporary position as an English teacher at her alma mater, James M. Bennett High School, but just as quickly as she had accepted, they called back and offered her a full-time position as an English teacher at Parkside High School. She immediately agreed, and at the start of the school year in 1983, Miss Alice Parsons joined the ranks of the teaching staff at Parkside High School. Among the faculty was Mrs. Dawn Neville, who had been Alice's sophomore-year homeroom teacher at James M. Bennett High School. Alice was now with her as an equal and they became instant friends. Dawn, and another teacher, Cheryl Pearce, helped Alice set up her classroom and get ready for the back to school rush.

The first year of teaching is often a trial by fire. There isn't much that can prepare a young teacher for having a room full of kids and finding oneself working without a net. Developing a rhythm, class after class, day after day, is no small task, especially under the weight of mountains of paperwork and administrative duties. That first year, everyone is learning, students and teacher alike. It is often a year filled with trepidation and broken expectations.

For Alice, the first years were tough. In some cases, she was only ten years older than her students and her naiveté was easy for them to see. They could tell she was nervous, and although many of her students thought she was nice and liked being in her class, there were some who sensed this anxiousness and took advantage. She had some rough classes, crowded with kids who unabashedly challenged authority, who talked back and didn't listen, who saw her perfect posture, conservative dress, and youthful face as a sign of her existence in a world that didn't include them. To drive the point home, one student even keyed her car.

In one of those tough classes sat Tyron Corbin, an attentive and extremely quiet young girl. On the first day of her freshman English class, in September 1984, she looked around the room and wasn't exactly sure how or why she was placed in group full of rowdy and insolent kids. Tyron's seat was at the front of the class, right next to her new teacher, Miss Parsons. The first day of school always presented a particular challenge for Tyron — that inevitable moment when the teachers would take roll and pronounce her name as "Tyrone." Yet, Miss Parsons didn't do that. Miss Parsons made a point to say her name correctly, and she would be the only one at Parkside to do so.

Miss Parsons quickly became one of her favorite teachers. Tyron admired her clothes and her poise and she loved the sound of her voice when she read to them, which she did often. Tyron appreciated her kindness and endless patience, especially when some of the students were pushing her and testing her. Miss Parsons refused to be bullied over the edge of her composure. That is, until the day a student in Tyron's class found a weak spot in her armor.

He called her a "virgin" in front of the entire class.

Tyron stared in horror as Miss Parsons's face flushed red. There was an awkward silence. The word hung in the air like a terrible odor, loathsome and repugnant. Miss Parsons sent him out of the room, but the damage was done. The class sat with their mouths agape and she retreated to her desk in the corner.

Tyron felt awful about what happened. Miss Parsons had only ever been nice to them, and perhaps surprisingly, she continued to be just as nice. Tyron often lingered after class to ask follow up questions on the assignments and Miss Parsons was happy to help and show her extra attention. It meant a lot to Tyron Corbin.

And so, despite the troublemakers and the missteps, Alice Parsons persevered. She did not quit. She taught the classics; she taught Shakespeare. She tasked her students with keeping journals and working their problems out on paper. In her creative writing class, she connected with another young student, Carl Thress, who loved to write. In his journal, he acknowledged his feelings of being painfully shy and his fear that he might never get over it and how it made him worry about finding a date. He was honest and vulnerable in his writing, and his teacher, Miss Alice Parsons, responded with kindness. In beautiful and precise cursive, she wrote in the margins of his notebook: "Don't worry about dating. You'll soon find someone who realizes how special you are!" In another note, on his entry about being shy, she wrote to Carl, "I used to be the same way. When you get older and more sure of yourself, you'll relax and the real, wonderful you will come out!" Even when Carl wrote that he was feeling discouraged, she told him not to give up. At the end of the year, in 1985, Carl Thress felt more confident in his writing and he was already hoping to find himself in another class with her.

Eventually Alice Parsons found her footing through the muck and mire. Was it the job Alice thought it would be? There's no way to know, but one thing is for sure: Alice figured out how to captain her classroom in the same way the strong women in her life had run ships of their own, just as Mary Belle had total command of their home and just as her old boss, Eileen, had organized the lobbying office. She found the reins and grasped them firmly in her hands. Alice, once a quiet little girl who instructed imaginary students, now stood at the front of her own classroon and stared into a sea of youthful faces and delivered her lessons.

•　•　•　•　•

Parkside High School became a home for Alice. It was the place where she found her calling as a teacher and it was the place where she met many of the women who became her closest friends. In addition to Dawn Neville and Cheryl Pearce, there was also Mary Starnes, Susan Westover-Huff, Colleen Dallam, Cindy Bennett, and Anne Collins who all befriended Alice.

Cindy Bennett had started teaching at Parkside the first year it opened in 1975 and met Alice when she came in 1983. Cindy was in the social studies department, which included subjects like history, government, geography, political science, and psychology. Through Dawn Neville, Cindy became acquainted with Alice and found her to be a conscientious co-worker. Cindy saw Alice spending unbelievable amounts of time grading papers and making notes in student journals only to leave the building with her arms full of more papers to finish up at home. Not every teacher was like this. Not every teacher put as much time and effort into giving students feedback. Cindy noticed when Alice became particularly aggravated with one male teacher who left the building every day without a single piece of paper in hand. Cindy heard Alice bemoan more than once, "If everyone would just do their job!" But Alice was not one to shirk her responsibilities, whether it was book reports or standing watch in the hallway or organizing the seniors for their graduation ceremony, whether the task at hand was assigned to her or not. Alice was sensible and fair and Cindy geniunely liked her.

Anne Collins started at Parkside two years after Alice, and her subject was history. She met Alice because they shared the same planning area, a workspace away from their classrooms and students. Anne and Alice hit it off despite Anne's disdain for fiction and overwrought literature. The ever-pragmatic Anne never saw the usefulness in those books, but she perked up when Alice invited her to speak about China and the revolution when Alice was teaching Pearl S. Buck's *The Good Earth*. They became friends even though they were just about as opposite as two women could be. Anne's classroom was sparse whereas Alice had what Anne called "visual clutter" with all her cat posters. If Anne was upset with her class, they sure knew it; Alice's students never saw her lose control. Even their teaching styles were different. Anne projected her voice across the classroom and sometimes down the hall; she was direct and commanding with her students. Anne was rapid fire: when she asked a question, sometimes the student barely had a chance to respond before Anne was interrupting with the right answer. Lecture. Q&A. Move it along. But Alice was different. In Alice, Anne saw a chess player, a teacher willing to take the time to set the kids up for the work at hand. She was patient, waiting until the perfect moment to say the perfect thing and then pull the lesson and her students into position. When Anne passed by Alice's classroom, the students were often the ones doing the talking, engaged and working through the material. It was a marvel to Anne.

Some teachers connected with their subject material and then worked to connect that material to the students. Alice, who unquestionably understood literature and composition, had a different approach. She connected with the kids and then used that connection to get them to understand the subject matter. From her desk in the corner of the room, she watched over her students while they busied themselves with required readings in their Perrine Literature textbooks or quick essays in their daily journals. In this classroom, she was the captain, clear-eyed and confident.

•   •   •   •   •

Bull's Eye

Don's Bella Donna was a bar on Eastern Shore Drive, just a quick walk (or an easy drunk stumble) from the Princeton Homes neighborhood where Jess lived. It was a blue collar dive, full of working guys looking for cold beer and maybe the warmth of a willing lady. Don, once the manager of a drug store in Cambridge, Maryland, had purchased the middle unit of a small commercial building. That unit was sandwiched between a store and a laundromat. The exterior was concrete blocks with a flat roof; inside, Don served pretty decent Italian food and a pitcher of cheap beer was only a buck or two.

As his neighbors vacated, Don acquired their spots and expanded so that he had room for a pool table and a couple of dart boards. Don's Bella Donna wasn't the finest drinking establishment in Salisbury. That title belonged to The Flying Club where attorneys and accountants, still in their suits and wingtips would drink martinis and scotch. Don's became a popular hole-in-the-wall for locals, like the union workers from the Dresser plant, electricians, construction workers, and even some of the braver college kids. Many of the guys who gathered there were single and starting out in the world, like Matthew Collier who was fresh out of high school and working for a furniture store, hauling sofas and Sealy Posturepedic mattresses. Matthew had graduated from Parkside High School in 1982 and had spent two teenage summers working for Pepsi Cola. Imagine his surprise when he walked into Don's Bella Donna in Salisbury and saw his old customer, Don, selling pints instead of prescriptions.

In 1984, Matthew met 31-year-old Jess Davis at Don's Bella Donna, and the two became quick friends, shooting pool, drinking beer, and throwing darts. They tossed tall tales back and forth, always trying to outdo the other. They had things in common like fishing, hunting, and being avid outdoorsmen. Beers and bullshit and a hearty slap on the back: a friendship built at Don's didn't need many more ingredients. Jess never failed to make Matthew laugh: he was always cracking jokes and telling crazy stories. Some of them were true. Like the time Matthew went to visit Jess and he saw firsthand that they really did use a yard rake to round up all the empty beer cans in the living room.

It wasn't all booze and darts and billards, though. With the ladies, Matthew watched Jess try his luck on a number of occasions. Althought Jess bragged about his success rate, Matthew was never quite sure it was all that Jess indicated. Was Jess some kind of irresistible Romeo? Not exactly. Lots of guys tried and failed and tried again; that's the nature of that particular game. Bragging was a given and only half-heartedly believed.

In Jess, Matthew found a lifelong friend, someone who never

failed to be there for him. If Matthew needed help, he didn't even have to ask. Jess was at the ready, a big smile and a helping hand. Theirs was a kinship forged in the smoky haze of a small town dive bar and it would last almost three decades, through the good times and the bad.

•   •   •   •   •

Italian Ice

On a warm summer day in the early 1980s, Gale looked down the aisle of the Fruitland A&P grocery store and did a double-take. There at the checkout counter was Alice with a strange man with a dark mustache. Her heart swelled up to see her friend. They had begun to drift apart as childhood friendships often do. A young woman can have a lifetime of experiences to fill in the gaps between her adolescence and adulthood — romantic partners, college, jobs, geography, hardship, discoveries of happiness and loss. To grow up is to change. This was true for Gale and Alice. Long gone were the innocent days of stealing the Parsons's whiskey and singing "American Pie" and giggling over yearbooks. They were women now.

While Alice had gone off to college and lived in D.C., Gale had stayed in Salisbury. She married Dean Dashiell in a private ceremony in November 1979. They didn't even tell his family, who would have wanted a wedding befitting the Dashiell name. Not even Dean's father knew. Socialite weddings are fancy and expensive by their very nature, replete with church bells and rose-filled bouquets and all the extravagant trimmings designed to impress the who's who guest list of the uptown crowd. Her farming family didn't have that kind of money or social standing and Gale didn't have that kind of patience. The whole notion of a lavish wedding felt wrong to them — Gale and Dean just wanted to get on with their lives together.

After their civil ceremony at the courthouse, Gale wrote a letter to tell Alice they had married. She detailed the peaceful day of their wedding: no family and friends, just the two of them making the solemn promises of husband and wife. Gale was happy and their life was good. When Alice wrote back, Gale sensed a tinge of disappointment. Gale wondered if perhaps she was upset because she wasn't invited, but literally no one had been invited. Or was there something else? Alice had been pulling away, or at least that's how it felt to Gale. Like the time Gale had been hospitalized for nearly a week at Peninsula General Hospital in Salisbury. She had reached out to Mary Belle to pass a message: would Alice come visit her? Mary Belle said she would tell Alice, and Gale waited for her friend … who never came.

Gale began to walk toward Alice and the man. They were buying little cups of Italian ice.

Alice looked up and met Gale's eyes, and in an instant, something changed. Alice didn't speak. She just stood at the register, unmoving as though rooted in place. Gale was confused, halted in the sea change, frozen in the unfamiliar silence that hung in the air between them. Gale glanced at the man with Alice. There was something about him that unnerved her. It was his eyes. Cold and blue. A chill went down her spine.

There was no attempt made for introductions. Not even a simple hello or a nod of a head. Although Alice was making it clear that she didn't want to speak to her, there wasn't anything malicious in Alice's eyes. Anger was not holding her back. Gale could not identify exactly what was happening. It was the fracture of a phantom limb: she could feel the hurt but she could not put her hands upon it. The distance between them had once felt glacial, expected and passive, like the slow erosion of a shoreline as they passed from childhood to womanhood, but in their bizarre supermarket encounter, the space between them erupted into a dark and wide canyon, and in mere milliseconds, it was impassable.

As Alice turned and walked away with the stranger, Gale's words died in her throat.

• • • • •

Until Death Do We Part

When Alice announced to her family that she and Jess planned to marry, there was a nearly palpable disappointment. Any hopes they had that Alice might see Jess for the cad he was were dashed against the rocks of their engagement. It was too late and now Jess was going to be a part of the family.

As the wedding plans began to move forward, something strange happened. Mary Belle called the printing company to discuss the invitations. She was informed that the wedding was on hold indefinitely. Unbeknownst to the family, the couple had called off the wedding, but Alice never said a word about it. Mary Belle was dumbstruck: *What was going on?*

Despite the gentle prodding from her family, Alice would not talk about it. There were questions. Was Alice second-guessing her choice, a man who was still trying his luck with other women down at Don's Bella Donna? Did Alice know or suspect as much? Had Jess backed out, broken her heart, lost his nerve? No one knew.

While she wouldn't talk to her family about it, Alice did confide in Dawn about the halted wedding. She said Jess told her he couldn't go through with it. Alice was crushed. She already had her dress. The couple took a little breather and spent some time apart. Dawn felt terrible for Alice, a young bride in love with a groom whose feet were ice cold.

Although her family was a little shocked, they were mostly relieved. This man did not love and honor Alice in his actions or words. It wasn't just as simple as his blue-collar job. It wasn't like Alice had to marry a doctor in order for them to approve. It was him. It was the kind of man he was. Her family breathed a collective sigh of relief. *Maybe the whole thing is over and he's out of her life for good,* they thought. Just like the Iranian guy, maybe this one would soon be a forgotten beau, a fortunate missed connection.

But their relief was short-lived. Alice announced several months later that the wedding was on again.

For her part, Alice was filled with trepidation. Would Jess go through with it this time? She implored him and he relented, reassuring her that he would. In the weeks leading up to the wedding, Alice was tense and nervous, so much so that she told Barrie that she couldn't even listen to the radio in the car. It made no sense. Alice who loved Elton John and Paul McCartney was driving to the high school every morning in complete silence and coming home the same way. Barrie knew this wasn't a good sign. She thought back to her own wedding to Mat and remembered how wonderful and exciting those times were. Yet with Alice, there was no hint of a blushing bride, happily anticipating and daydreaming of her wedding. All of it felt wrong. Barrie wanted to ask her sister, *doesn't this tell you something?*

Alice was forging ahead with her plans to marry Jess. For better or worse, she loved him and she was not going to give him up.

Was there a part of Alice that thought he was the best she could do? Was there a part of Alice unwilling to find out? And in settling for Jess, could she avoid the small town stigma of a school teacher nearing her 30s and having her name whispered with words like "old maid?" With Jess, there was possibility. She could meet the expectations, follow in the footsteps of the women before her. She could achieve the status her mother and sisters had. Equal in marriage. She could create a home and family of her own where there would be evening cocktails and festive holiday spreads. The entire dream was just within her reach … as long as they could make it to the altar.

· · · · ·

The wedding was set for the evening of July 27th, 1985. Everything was coming together this time, and Jess had assured her that he was going to be there. He would not let her down a second time. Theirs was a beautiful candlelight ceremony at the country church in Allen, the one she and her family had attended faithfully for decades. Alice's bridal party was a small but intimate one — her sisters, Barrie and Ellen, as well as Jess's sister, Patricia. Ellen's daughter, Kim, was the maid of honor; Barrie's daughter, Casey, was the flower girl. They wore pearls and long rose taffeta skirts with sheer ivory blouses. In each of their arms, they carried ivory silk flowers and a single, long stem pink rose. Kim's beau, Jay Ragains, was one of the ushers in the groom's party.

Soon, it was time for the ceremony. Alice and her father rode together in the limousine. Casey could tell his daughter was a frightful ball of nerves. It tore him up to see her this way. *What could he do?* As they headed toward the church, Casey asked the driver to pull over at the Parsons home. While Alice waited, he went inside and made her a martini. Perhaps a drink might help ease her mind, allow her to shake off at least some of the anxieties she was feeling. Casey came back to the limousine, handed her a strong martini, and said gently, "Get yourself together now. He showed up. The hard part is over."

Alice, in her wedding dress with a martini in hand, sat next to her father and steeled her nerves for what was next.

Everything had come to this moment. She arrived at the country church, now decorated in palms, pink and ivory gladioli, carnations, and roses. The candles were lit and the congregation was enchanted as Alice Elizabeth Parsons slowly walked down the aisle in a long gown of white taffeta, covered in Alencon lace and little pearls. In her hands she carried a bouquet of freesia, ivory carnations, and pink sweetheart roses. She was a pure vision.

Alice, the reserved young girl who had once shied away from her own prom, changed with each step toward the altar, toward him. Alice's inexperience no longer mattered; hidden and virginal under a veil trimmed in white flowers, she walked with the poise of a woman. Her likeness was the very thing of a little girl's dreams. Alice was beautiful, absolutely stunning. Her lips parted in a knowing smile and her cheeks blushed; her brown hair was swept back under a crown of pearls, revealing a slender neck and strong shoulders. Under the sequins and trimmed bodice and wispy veil, there wasn't a trace of her awkwardness, no hints of her reservations, no cracks in her lovely armor, nothing but a bride so gentle and soft.

Elsewhere in the congregation, there were a few concerned looks exchanged and brows furrowed. Barrie, who also needed a stiff drink before the ceremony, held her breath as the reverend said, "Does anyone see just cause why these two should not be married?" Barrie caught the eye of her husband, Mat, and they shared the tense silence. She didn't say a word. No one did. After all, wasn't this what Alice wanted?

At the end of the church aisle lined in fragrant flowers and flickering candles, surrounded by family and friends, in front of the Father, Son, and the Holy Ghost, she took Jess's hand and the spell was cast. In an instant, Alice was a woman transformed.

The couple exchanged gold rings and vowed to love each other until death and sealed that promise with a kiss. And then, hand in hand with her new husband, Alice Parsons emerged from the green gabled country church as Mrs. Alice Davis.

Part II

"Lord, we know what we are, but know not what we may be."

HAMLET
ACT IV, SCENE V

First Impressions

On the first day of school in September 1996, I entered Parkside High School as a senior and looking like a movie extra from *Dazed and Confused*: dark green corduroy pants rolled up at the cuffs to reveal my brown leather Birkenstock sandals and a white v-neck cotton shirt — a Hanes multipack special like my grandfather would have worn. Around my neck was a yin and yang pendant strung on a woven hemp cord purchased from a head shop I frequented on the boardwalk in Ocean City, Maryland. My long blonde hair was parted down the middle, framing a freckled face that rarely saw makeup. I wore a sterling silver ring on my right thumb. A hint of patchouli and vanilla announced my arrival.

Much to my mother's consternation, I had blossomed into the Hendrix and Zeppelin, terrible-poetry-writing, wanna-be flower child phase of my late teenage years. I kept a thrift store paperback of Hemingway's *The Old Man and The Sea* on my nightside table, right next to my incense burner and a leather bound journal filled with overwrought stanzas and a few daisies and black-eyed Susans pressed between the pages. Teenage years are full of angst and upheaval, but I was searching for something ... I wanted a sense of calm, of balance. Wasn't that the thing about hippies? All peace and love and easy going? My heart was desperate for it.

Despite my appearance, I wasn't a total bohemian. By that first day of school, I was already the co-captain of the varsity volleyball team, and while certainly not the smartest kid in the building, I was a college bound member of the National Honor Society. My sights were already set on Washington College, a small liberal arts college in Chestertown, Maryland. Their writing program was renowned and they had the Sophie Kerr Prize, the largest undergraduate literary award in the country. But before I could get there, I had to pull off a successful senior year. My schedule was full of Advanced Placement classes, designed to prepare high school students for college. For me, there was AP Calculus with Ms. Melissa Napoleon, AP US History with Ms. Anne Collins, AP Government with Mrs. Cindy Bennett, AP World History with Mrs. Colleen Dallam, and AP English with Mrs. Alice Davis.

Before I strolled into Mrs. Davis's classroom, I could feel my nerves setting themselves on fire. She had a reputation among the students at Parkside that fell just short of eating kids for breakfast. Tough. No nonsense. No one was going to get an easy A. There were whispers that she didn't make exceptions for student-athletes who had to leave early for away games. *Uh oh.* That classroom, lined with posters of cats and kittens, was ruled by a tigress. She made her students work hard and she expected the best while her students feared the worst. I was one of them.

As I took my seat in the front of the class beside the overhead projector cart, I worried about failure. *Could I make it in this class?* Glancing around the room revealed that the brightest and smartest kids in the entire senior class were here. There was Barbara Kiviat who, just months later, would be our valedictorian and then head off to Johns Hopkins. A few rows back was Leslie Cooley who was the exact thing every girl wanted to be: smart, athletic, pretty, and popular. These were future lawyers and doctors. My eyes bounced from one smart kid to another even smarter kid. While I had been taking standard English classes, most of the kids who now surrounded me had always been together in the advanced English class.

I could feel myself beginning to spiral into self-doubt and negativity. Although I had the look of a laid-back, hippie child, I had a secret: I struggled with anxiety. I was haunted by it. Sports were a release for much of the tension within me, but that only worked outside the classroom. So I reached for another answer: the green agate worry stone in my pocket. I carried it with me wherever I went, twiddling it in my fingers and running my thumb obsessively over its smooth surface. It was a comfort and a release. I reached for it — my stomach full of panicked butterflies as I realized that my seat for the remainder of the year was going to be the one that was right next to *her.*

I glanced up at Mrs. Davis. The butterflies in my stomach swarmed up into my throat. She was tall and stood ramrod straight, which gave the impression that she was towering over me. I felt an immediate and unspoken command in that. Curiosity got the better of me and I studied her. Her eyes were blue like the sky on a crisp autumn morning. Beautiful, actually. She had a kind face with cherubic cheeks, framed by soft brown hair that danced on her shoulders. And when she spoke, there was something in her voice — almost like a soft hum or a lightness to her cadence that interrupted the obsessive and anxious thoughts gnawing their way through my brain. Although authoritative in posture, she wasn't exactly the harsh legend I had come to fear.

I liked her.

My eyes took a quick inventory. The walls of her classroom were plastered in posters of kittens and cats. A calico kitten reading a book. A cat sitting on a white drop cloth with open cans of red and yellow paint. The picture of the tiger emerging from a river: it was a close up of its side profile, as though it was peeking its head up like a submarine periscope to survey its environs. A big black and red *Revenge of the Jedi* poster. Underneath that, a multi-color one that read, "This is the week that Beatlemania was!"

What an odd mix, I thought.

In front of my desk was another poster called "The Procrastinator's Creed" featuring a list of commandments and a two-headed turtle. Number 4 was a gem: "I shall meet all of my deadlines directly in proportion to the amount of bodily injury I could expect to receive from missing them."

Uh oh. I shifted my eyes to the next poster which reminded me that "Learning Lasts A Lifetime!"

While she was taking attendance, I kept fiddling with the green agate worry stone, running my thumb again and again over its smooth surface to ease my nerves and my mind. And then I dropped it. As it clanged and banged on the metal legs of my desk and rattled its way to the floor, silence filled the room. My heart seized up inside my chest. Mrs. Davis paused in the middle of roll call.

As I bent down to pick it up, I swear I could almost feel her eyes on the back of my head. I did not look up. I just shoved the stone back into the pocket of my thrift-store pants and prepared myself for a very, very long year.

. . . . . .

Parkside: Home of the Rams

Parkside High School opened in 1975 and its halls smacked of every color iconic to that disco decade: we had tangerine orange lockers, beige walls, chocolate brown chalkboard panels, even that weird avocado green appeared in the hues of the carpet. It was the same color scheme as my mother's Tupperware collection and my grandmother's faux-tile kitchen linoleum.

Outside the cafeteria, vertical stripes of baby blue and butter yellow ceramic tiles adorned the hallway, which led down to the gym and auditorium, past the oversized trophy case and onward to the art, choir, band, and shop rooms. Tiny metal flecks and stoney-shards flashed in the industrial white tile flooring. Fluorescent lights buzzed overhead, interspersed with square acoustic tiles in the ceiling. Our school colors were white, black, and Kelly green.

It was a psychedelic kaleidoscope, a smash of this and that from a commercial painter's palette.

Parkside had an unusual design. One of the first things a passerby might notice about our two-story school was the lack of windows, which earned the school an unfortunate moniker among the students: "Parkside Prison." Inside, the design was reminiscent of the popular open-floor plan concepts of the 1970s. The downstairs classrooms had no interior doors, just a gap in the walls, giving each room the feel of a yawning alcove. Every classroom in the school, despite being windowless, had an exterior door with a sliver of a window. It was a strange set-up, but we had one great advantage: air conditioning, an uncommon luxury in Wicomico County schools. During May and June on the Eastern Shore of Maryland, temperatures begin to climb and the humidity can be stifling. The air grows so thick with moisture that you can see a haze on the horizon. If the weather became unbearable, the other county schools would close, and when that happened, the Parkside kids also got out of school. This seemed counter-intuitive: someone saw fit to give us air-conditioning but still let us go home when the other schools got too hot. I often thought back to my days at the old James M. Bennett Middle School when the teachers kept the lights off in the classrooms and stationed box fans around the room to move the stagnant air. The backs of our thighs stuck to the plastic chairs; rivers of sweat ran down our temples and necks and into our t-shirts. At Parkside, we didn't have that problem but we still prayed for hot days because we could think of a hundred better things to do with our time on warm spring afternoons.

The other feather in our cap was our planetarium — a real and fully functional planetarium with the reclining seats — and it was the only one on the Delmarva Peninsula. Students from all over came to Parkside for field trips. Even students at the other county high schools who could drive were allowed to come to Parkside to take Astronomy as an elective. It was a popular course, taught by Mr. Goodyear who used to play "Here Comes the Sun" by The Beatles as an orange spot arose in the darkness and swept overhead. When I took Astronomy, I sat next to a kid who used to smoke weed in his beat-up station wagon before coming into class.

"This," he used to croak as we watched stars appear overhead, "is so awesome."

I couldn't argue with that.

Parkside was just a regular, run-of-the-mill high school. A group of guys played hacky sack outside on the concrete pad by the cafeteria doors. Lunch was loud and smelled of Sysco and Otis Spunkmeyer cookies. The roof often leaked and the custodians caught the rain water in garbage cans. During one particularly bad stretch of weather, they made a huge slip-and-slide from the ceiling to the floor with plastic sheeting. The pep rallies featured our mascot, Randy the Ram. While it may seem like someone chose livestock to represent a high school in a predominately rural county, our mascot was actually an homage to Royd A. Mahaffey, the county school superintendent. His initials: RAM. We made the best of it, though: the newspaper was *The RamPage* and the student literary magazine was *The Ramazine*. (I was a member of its editorial staff in 1996.) The word *Aries* was featured prominently on the front of the yearbook, usually in a metallic foil to make it fancy. The other high schools were the Mardela Warriors, the Wicomico Indians, and the Bennett Clippers. Although we were all rivals, there was one thing just about every student could agree on: we were all glad we weren't the Trojans from Kent County, Maryland.

In the petri dish of high school, that Erlenmeyer flask of hormones and awkwardness, the kids at Parkside divided themselves in all the canonical ways. The freshman and sophomores tried to navigate their way in a world where the rules were made up by adults and upperclassmen. Athletes and thespians, nerds and rednecks. We had every cliché category. I found myself occupying that middle space in the Venn Diagram of high school classification: a hippie girl who was proficient in sports and above average at academics. But we were all a little weird, in one way or another, and while some kids bravely wore it like a badge of honor, the rest of us hid behind designer jeans and varsity jackets or Birkenstocks and patchouli.

These were the days before social media and cell phones. The big deal then was to carry a beeper and have your own telephone in your bedroom. These were the years before Columbine, before surveillance cameras dotted the hallways. The greatest scandal was when the Driver's Education teacher fell asleep in class, some of the braver students used to sneak out and head down to the Amoco gas station on the corner for Jolt colas and discount cigarettes. Cutting class was a cinch if you had the right teacher.

Maybe it was a little simpler or maybe time just allows me to remember things that way.

•   •   •   •   •

A Sisterhood

At Parkside, Alice found a true camaraderie with other teachers. During their planning periods and lunch breaks, they shared anecdotes about their students as well as stories of their husbands and their own children. The women bonded. They could understand the daily ups and downs of the teaching grind because they were living it themselves. Theirs was the kind of unique kinship one develops with people in shared vocations. Cops have it. Nurses have it. Bartenders and wait staff have it. The common experience of their jobs made for certain inside jokes, established lingo, and a behind-the-scenes sorority.

Their sisterhood extended beyond the walls of Parkside. Alice and Jess became close with Dawn Neville and her husband, Bill, as well as with Cheryl Pearce and her husband, George, who was also a teacher at Parkside. The three couples took trips together and spent weekends boating on the Wicomico River, drinking and laughing. The Pearces' pontoon boat served as a floating tiki bar, and Alice's drink of choice was always the vodka martini. Often Jess and Alice drank heavily on the boat rides and started to earn a bit of a reputation for it. The other couples started to see Jess's uproarious nature and how quickly he could shift from jovial to angry. Once, down at the harbor in Mount Vernon, Maryland, Jess nearly got into a fist fight with a man who, according to Jess, had been following him because of his claims over finding a dead mouse in his Coke bottle. It was impulsive and hotheaded, like the time Jess minorly vandalized a local restaurant called Curley's Garage. It was a popular, novelty eatery in Salisbury; the interior was decorated like a car garage with vintage signs and pumps, hubcaps and car parts on the walls. Even the menu followed the motif: you could order a Studeburger with peppers and onions and wash it down with a mixed drink like Anti-Freeze or Windshield Wiper Fluid. As Bill and Jess were walking out after eating dinner, Jess stopped and grabbed ahold of one of the decorations affixed to the wall. He yanked it off and handed it to a speechless Bill. Jess grinned broadly and said, "Here! Have this!" Early on, Bill learned that, for Jess Davis, crossing the line was a trifle.

The Nevilles continued a close relationship with Alice and Jess. They would frequently go down to Alice's uncle's beach house at Brick Landing Plantation in North Carolina. They'd stay for a week and enjoy the amenities. At the pool, Jess would perform, strutting around like a banty rooster and getting everyone worked up. Alice frequently had to tone him down, like the time when he nearly got into a shouting fight with another guest who was trying to enjoy the pool with his family. In another episode, there was the night at a restaurant in Myrtle Beach when Jess told their waitress that Bill Neville was the governor of Maryland. Bill, playing along for a moment, said, "Yes, and he's my aide-de-camp." The young waitress believed the fib and brought the manager over to welcome the "governor." For Dawn, it was awkward and unnecessary, and she was a little taken aback when she looked at Alice who was in absolute hysterics over the situation.

The scene left Dawn wondering, *why does Alice find him so funny?* For some measure of an answer, she looked to their interactions. They appeared as a loving couple. When Jess teased Alice, he'd playfully tug on her hair or shake the back of her head with his hand. In response, Alice would joke, "Jess Davis, you're an asshole." To which, Jess would pause mid-laugh and say, "Now now, that's Mr. Asshole to you!" They bantered back and forth like any married couple; he flattered her and she laughed at his silliness. To Dawn, Alice had married a big, boisterous boy who needed a constant audience and an occasional mother. For every moment in which Alice complained about an unruly student, Dawn just shook her head as if to say *but you married that kid, Alice.* He was a handful, for sure, but Alice didn't seem to mind. She was always right there, next to him, laughing at his jokes or hushing him or soothing his bruised ego. She was always there, supporting him and loving him no matter the circumstance or mood, no matter what he had done.

While Jess's behavior sometimes vacillated between over-the-top and confrontational, there were moments of genuine and heartfelt expression. Just as quickly as he would try to shock her friends, he would also help them. When Colleen Dallam's husband passed away, Jess became a mentor to her oldest son, Travis, who was just 12. The young boy had inherited his father's hunting gene and Jess Davis, being an avid hunter and outdoorsman, found a way to connect with him. They went hunting together. Jess became a sincere and avuncular figure to Travis, and in turn, Travis looked up to Jess, a man who spent countless hours in the forests with him, teaching him, talking with him, and looking after him. Alice invited Colleen and her boys to their home for Thanksgiving and Christmas, starting a new tradition for both families. It was a difficult time for Colleen and her boys made easier by the comforting friendship of Alice and Jess Davis.

In Jess, Colleen and her sons saw a passionate, animated man who loved to crack jokes and would talk faster and faster as he got riled up in conversation. Jess would tell funny stories about Travis, and he nearly burst with pride when the young man became a police officer. Sure, he was a little rough, but Jess was the kind of man who called his wife "dear" and complimented her cooking. Colleen's mind and heart were put to ease because her sons had a positive male figure in their lives.

On summer breaks, Alice and Colleen joined the other teachers for lunch dates at places like Market Street Inn in Salisbury and Sunset Grill in West Ocean City. Sometimes they commemorated the afternoon with a photograph and in every single one of them, each woman is smiling. The lives of these women were intertwined. They shared holidays, birthdays, and life milestones together. At Cindy Bennett's daughter's wedding, someone snapped a photograph of Alice and Jess in the congregation. She had her arm wrapped around him and a broad, happy smile upon her face; Jess's arms were crossed in front of his barrel-round chest and his lips were pressed together in a half-smirk.

Each year brought a new set of students, faces, and personalities to learn and, in some cases, contend with. The general rule of thumb is to keep a safe emotional distance. Don't get overly involved and stay as objective as possible. Be careful of forming intimate personal bonds with students. Navigating that path could be delicate and possibly dangerous. After all, you're a teacher, not a parent or a social worker or a therapist. Balance sensitivity with formality and keep all boundaries in place. It's a good protocol, but not every teacher adheres to it.

Alice, of course, followed her own set of rules when it came to what was right and necessary for her students. The balance was not about tiptoeing within administrative guidelines, but about the individual in front of her. Should she listen or challenge? What did this student need to hear? What did she want to say to them? Tone and language and timing: with her students, Alice's instincts were rarely wrong.

• • • • •

Shakespeare and Heartache

In the beginning of the school year, my confidence was next to nil. Every time I walked into Mrs. Davis's room, I felt the tension of her expectations, of my insecurities, of the secrets I carried with me. The truth as I saw it: I wasn't smart enough for her class and I worried she would see that. English had always been my favorite subject and I had always loved to read and write, but my early successes were forged in less challenging classrooms. Writing had become cathartic for me. The things I kept inside, the things that ate me alive could all be worked out on paper. In those blue ink scribbles on white pages, I found a way to understand my world and myself … but even then, I knew there was difference between loving to write and actually being good at it.

I learned it was impossible to hide from Mrs. Davis. She looked out over her classroom as a lioness might survey the savannah. She sized us up, assessing our individual capabilities and short-comings. What motivated us? What were we responding to in the lessons? She quickly discovered that I loved to write and, much to my surprise, she was encouraging and kind about it. During one assignment, she gave me Maya Angelou's *I Know Why the Caged Bird Sings* and I was captivated by it. The book was transformative, like turning on a light in a dark room; up to that point, school had mostly consisted of works like *The Good Earth*, *The Crucible*, and *The Scarlet Letter*. This book felt accessible and real to me in a way those other ones hadn't. Mrs. Davis knew good writing and in handing me that book, she ensured I would too. My journals began to fill faster and faster, pages upon pages of poems and short essays and daily notes as I started down the path of understanding my own identity. I wrote and I wrote and I wrote, and with Mrs. Davis as an early champion, my self-doubt began to lessen its grip.

Our Shakespeare segment must have been her favorite: *Hamlet* and *MacBeth*. And no one in the room was more excited for it than Mrs. Davis. She could quote his sonnets like her students could rhyme off the lyrics to "California Love" by Tupac Shakur. She scrutinized the plot line of the star-crossed lovers Romeo and Juliet the way my friends agonized over Angela and Jordan on *My So-Called Life* or Ross and Rachel on *Friends*. She had a mind for his language, the wit and charm and those turns of phrase and plot; she appreciated his way of seeing into and then right through a scene. She loved it, and her love inspired us. We followed along.

After we read, dissected, and digested *MacBeth*, she organized a field trip for her classes to see a production at the University of Maryland Eastern Shore in Princess Anne. Field trips were exciting but this one was special. We were going to see a real performance of what we had just studied. Our local paper, *The Daily Times*, featured a short story about our field trip. The reporter quoted one student, Donnell Cole, as saying he felt the performance didn't place enough emphasis on some vital parts of the play. At the end of the article, the reporter noted that Mrs. Davis's students lamented the "lack of passion" put forward by the actors. That was a revelation unto itself: somehow, someway, she made a classroom full of 20th century 17-year-olds fall in love with the ancient bones of Shakespeare.

Forever frozen in my memory, or perhaps seared is a better word, is one particular interlude from our dissection of *Hamlet*. Mrs. Davis was reading from Act 1, Scene 5, and she came to the line, "O most pernicious woman!" This is the moment in the play when the ghost of Hamlet's father, the old king, tells Hamlet that his uncle Claudius is the one who murdered him and then married the Queen. It is a moment of revelation. Hamlet is disgusted and torn and he first directs his anger at his mother — "O most pernicious woman!"

As she delivered the line, she was grinning and triumphant, as though the very words themselves were delicious. I was spellbound. Her blue eyes sparkled under the overhead lights. Her voice punctuated the reading, loud and clear and full of delight. The "s" in pernicious lingered on her lips; she punched with "woman." It is no wonder we lamented those actors. They just didn't have it in them the way she did.

Mrs. Davis was special. Beyond the demands and rigors of her class, beyond the critical essays and heaps of homework she assigned, there was something else. I could see it in her — a genuine kindness in her eyes, a gentleness in her hands, a preternatural sensitivity to us akin to a sixth sense. Looking up at Mrs. Davis, I could see there was more to her than the hallway rumors. She wasn't awful or tyrannical. The intimidation I had felt was my own, nothing manufactured by her.

But just as my fear of Mrs. Davis was subsiding, another terror began to take shape: my mother's kidneys were failing.

• • • • •

During my junior year, my mother, Jacki, had decided to redo our 1970s kitchen. The dark brown cabinets and golden formica countertops with matching paisley linoleum along with the mustard yellow fridge and stove all received their marching orders. It was time for the past to meet the present. Our new setup: cabinets painted in rustic French blue with distress marks, faux granite formica countertops in a color scheme called "Butternut Squash," stainless steel appliances, and new laminate cherry wood floors. When it was finished, it was gorgeous—my mother being a combination of Bob Villa and Martha Stewart.

One of the side projects involved refinishing an antique washstand, an heirloom from her grandfather. Someone in our family had painted it an unflattering pea soup green, but some of the lacquer was beginning to flake off and as it did, my mother realized underneath that stale veneer was the beautiful grain of old walnut. She purchased an extremely potent paint remover, opened every window, turned on the ceiling fan, and set to work.

The next morning, she was vomiting profusely and spiking a fever. Her cheeks were flushed and pink. Her joints, visibly swollen, ached with every movement. We weren't exactly sure what was going on. She didn't know either. *Perhaps some kind of allergic response?* Within a few days, the symptoms were gone. The kitchen was finished and the wooden washstand was returned to its former, stunning glory. Life in our house seemed to return to normal.

Only it wasn't.

Something was wrong with my mother and she knew it. She was an ICU-trained nurse who was the Assistant Manager of the Respiratory Department at Peninsula Regional Medical Center. When she went to the doctor, the test results showed there was significant damage to her kidneys. What followed next, over the course of several months, spilling into my senior year of high school, was a mind-wrecking tailspin: an onset of severe diabetes, renal failure, steroids, total hair loss, constant nausea, weight gain, and a long list of other indignities and complications.

Something changed within me during those days. Every morning, I watched her dress for work, do her make-up, put on her wig, and head off to her full-time job. In the evenings, she cooked dinner, paid the bills, straightened up the house, and helped us with homework. She even stood in as coach for my little sister's softball team upon learning the girls had no one at the helm. She was always pushing forward and refusing to stop. Sympathy was unacceptable to her. Through her silent suffering, she nurtured us and raised us without complaining and without letting her guard down for fear we'd glimpse the truth about her condition and be afraid.

In truth, she was afraid. Although she wasn't yet at the point of dialysis, the drug treatments were not what we hoped for: they may have been helping, but they also seemed to be causing an equal number of ill side-effects. By the time my senior year had begun, her blood sugars hit toxic levels. Lumps burgeoned from her body. She wasn't getting better and she knew it.

On December 26th, 1996, my mother went for her first kidney biopsy. I remember seeing her in the hospital room, laying on her belly with the blue gown draped across her back. She looked at me and told me it would be OK, to go have a seat in the waiting room and keep my little sister company. The white antiseptic hallways of the hospital began to narrow as I walked away from her. The only safety net my sister and I had was slipping out from under us. We could not lose her. A hard knot formed in my throat.

A few days later, she came home from work, took off her wig, and laid her head in my lap. I started to massage her bare scalp while I finally worked up the nerve to ask her if she knew anything yet. Her blue eyes were steady, but full of things I couldn't yet read. She said the doctors told her they were running out of ideas. She closed her eyes. My fingers kept moving in small, slow circles where her once dark hair, full of tight curls and hairspray, now gave way to a barren landscape of yellow skin and red bumps. She took a deep breath and let out a sigh that froze me, "They say I may likely die from this."

I couldn't even bring myself to ask how long we had. I thought of my little sister.

I was 17. And terrified.

•   •   •   ◦   ◦

Back at school, there was work to do. Mrs. Davis had assigned our class an essay on "Paul's Case," a short story by Willa Cather. The story revolves around a young man who is struggling at home, at school, and mostly within himself. He sees his current middle-class life as beneath him, and he longs for the stage and bright lights, glitz and glamour, art and sophistication. But all those things are beyond his reach and so he steals money from his job and runs away. For a short time, he lives the life he desires, but the story culminates in his suicide because he can no longer face the consequences of his actions and the reality of his simple position in the world.

As I read the story, I felt disgusted with Paul who, in my righteous, teenaged opinion, was a shallow, narcissistic twit with a vainglorious attitude. He was lazy and infuriating; he was the kind of kid who I could easily imagine skipping out on a group assignment but still demanding he get an "A" anyway. I did not like him and I was irritated about having to waste my time on him. The assignment was straightforward but it felt like an insult: reading it was enough, honestly, but now Mrs. Davis wanted us to write an essay about this jerk?

I couldn't do it. Everything in my head and my heart kept coming back to my mother, and I was running out of the patience and energy required to keep moving forward.

My mother was the glue holding our family together. She was the only reason we had any resemblance of normalcy at all. My father, although present in the house, was a shift-working ghost whose multiple affairs had set the sides: us versus him. Our relationship had once been loving and happy, but had become fraught with frustration brought about by his mercurial nature. My mother set the pace: get up, get ready, face the day, do your work, and wash your hands before dinner. Regardless of the pain and exhaustion, she didn't flinch and she didn't stop, and so my little sister and I felt we couldn't either. We followed her lead. We kept the fear and hurt and anger inside, pushed way down deep, while we presented smiling faces to the world at large.

But I am not built like my lionhearted mother or even my plucky little sister. Where they have the spines made of steel, I am made of something else. I am the wood of a willow tree, ever flexing and bending. My courage often leaves me wanting. In those days of her sickness, I knew I needed an unflinching face full of resolve, but I was aching and I was heading for a breakdown. The toll of a rigorous academic courseload and my athletic schedule only amplified the constant anxiety that my mother was slipping away from me. I was running almost all the time. I ran so much that my feet blistered and bled. In those bloody shoes, I saw my own personal violence: hurt one thing to avoid feeling another hurtful thing. The searing of my soles replaced the panic of my mind.

In the evenings, after school and practice, I'd come home and find my mother, bald and plump, busying herself in the kitchen. I would see her at the new stainless steel stove and realize she was nearly unrecognizable to me. Upstairs, her wig rested on a mannequin head on the dresser in her bedroom. She did not cry. She did not complain. Which made me feel like I had little right do so either. But something in me was giving out. No matter how much I ran or how much I wrote, I could not keep up.

I was falling apart. And the straw to break my back? That essay in Mrs. Davis's AP English class.

• • • • •

As the deadline for the paper approached, I had nothing left to give. My bloody running shoes and my agate worry stone no longer held any respite. I withdrew. And then the day came to turn in my essay.

All the students were passing their papers forward. I collected the bundle passed to me and handed it to Mrs. Davis. She eyeballed the stack. "Where is yours?"

"I don't have it." I glanced up and caught her eyes searching me. I quickly looked away.

"What do you mean you don't have it?"

"I don't have it, and I'm not going to have it." I kept my eyes down.

There was a sharp sensation in my stomach like a knife being drawn upwards from my navel — I was disobeying authority. I was finally pushing back against the tidal wave of unfair things that had been crashing down on me. Sick of being pushed around by one awful circumstance after another, I was drowning in the tears I could not shed. No, I had had enough and I refused to give in. Even if it was only a dumb essay. I felt free.

Until I looked at her face. I only saw disappointment and concern. She almost looked hurt. Mrs. Davis turned away from me.

Oh no, what have I done?

The once sharp sensation of rebellion took a hard left into deep regret and guilt.

As the bell rang, she called my name. "Come here, please."

I knew I had it coming. Of all things, she was the wrong teacher for this kind of idiotic stunt. I chose poorly and I knew she was about to let me know she didn't suffer fools gladly.

Standing in front of her, I forced myself to look up. That was the least I could do. Her blue eyes were equal parts intense and inquisitive: "Stephanie, what's going on with you? Are you alright?"

Months of agony, fear, anger, and sheer exhaustion bubbled up to the surface. I couldn't hold it in any longer. My eyes welled up with tears and the dam let loose. And I finally spoke, "No, Mrs. Davis … I'm not okay."

With that admission, I broke open. I told her about my mother. About my fear of her dying. About what the doctors said. About being scared every moment of every day. About what it was like at home. About how I wasn't prepared for any of it. I let it all go. As I cried, she opened her arms and I fell into her warm embrace. I sobbed against her. "I'm just so scared, Mrs. Davis."

"I know. I know. It'll be okay." Her arms tightened around me. One hand rubbed my back.

Out it came. Every bit of the poison.

There in that moment, something incredible happened to me. This woman, who had once so intimidated me on the first day of school, was now showing me such tenderness and empathy. She innately understood what I needed. I was a scared kid who needed refuge. She could give that. And she did.

She also gave me a couple of extra days to finish my paper. And I did.

• • • • •

I started going to her classroom every chance I could, not just English class. I came during my study hall, after school, before practice. Sometimes, I'd just walk by her room between classes as the halls flooded with acne-faced kids hustling to their lockers, passing love notes, and sneaking off for smoke breaks outside the cafeteria. I yearned for the comfort I felt when I was close to her. With each visit, she listened to me and she let me cry; her kindness was a balm to my wounds. Once I had confessed everything to Mrs. Davis, I didn't need to hurt myself as much. I bandaged the blisters on my feet. And despite still being terrified of my mother's illness, I felt better. There was someone listening to me. I had a safe place to go where I could release all the fear and doubt and anger. Mrs. Davis helped me make peace with it.

But in her classroom, I had to work. Just because she understood what I was going through did not mean I got a pass. Oh no, work was necessary and there was no such thing as a valid excuse or a reason to quit. There was no use in feeling sorry for myself. Yes, there were difficulties in my life but she was not willing to allow me to skate. Instead, she leaned on me a little harder, and in doing so, she taught me a great lesson: work through the heartache; *work because of the heartache.*

Alice Davis saved me.

Although straight-laced and reserved, she encouraged the writing nonconformist in me, even when my essays went against her natural grain. Once I wrote a paper arguing for the legalization of marijuana. That one made her eyes roll. She knew I was just trying to rile her up, playfully of course, and I knew she'd never give into such nonsense, but, as always, she judged me on the merits of my work and ability, not the content of my irreverent high school essays. The weed term paper did not get my highest marks in her class.

As graduation approached so did the final thesis paper. Each senior chose their topic and then had to follow through on the research, the outline, and the revisions. Miniature mountains of index cards and a graveyard of highlighters. Most seniors loathed the project, but I relished every second of it. I chose to write about historic downtown Salisbury, documenting its evolution from the time of the Native Americans to present-day revitalization efforts. Mrs. Davis scrutinized my work. Her red pen tore through swaths of my early drafts. I buckled down, determined to ace this last paper, this last moment to shine in her class. And there was an additional incentive: whoever wrote the best thesis might win the Thomas H. Williams Old Home Prize at the Senior Awards ceremony. Wouldn't that make her proud of me? I set my eyes on the prize.

With each draft, I was convinced this was going to be the one to wow her, but every single one came back wounded and stained from her red pen. More index cards. More books. More research and interviews with old folks. Edits upon edits. I kept working. When the due date arrived, I had my senior thesis in hand, typed and bound. I wouldn't make that stupid mistake twice. Not with her. I had learned my lesson.

In addition to the senior thesis, there was an even bigger event looming on the horizon — prom. We chose "Tahitian Moons" as our theme, which was a bit laughable as only a handful of kids could have even picked out Tahiti on a map. We decorated the Normandy Room of the Wicomico Youth and Civic Center in lattice work and brightly colored paper flowers. Silvery moons and stars dangled from the ceiling. A stage with an arch and a runway was erected in the main room of the Civic Center where the Grand March would be held. On the night of April 25th, 1997, the seniors strutted, arm in arm with our dates, couple by couple, down the lit catwalk for the Grand March to the cheers of our families and the teachers who came to see us in our sequins and beads and tuxedos and top hats. As each couple was announced, the audience, seated in the darkened auditorium, erupted with applause. We were shining.

As soon as Grand March ended and just before the dance began, we filed out into the lobby of the building. I scanned hundreds of faces until I locked onto my mother's eyes and then right behind her, Mrs. Davis. I wanted to see them both because I wanted to introduce them. These two incredible, strong women ... I loved them both. They smiled at me and they smiled at each other. And my mother had reason to smile: she had been accepted into a kidney research program at Johns Hopkins in Baltimore. We had hope.

After hugging my mother and then Mrs. Davis, I turned to my sister, Kristen, who came along as the date of a friend of mine. It was time to celebrate. We grabbed the hands of our dates and ran off to dance in the shadows under cutout moons and stars. We laughed and twirled and sang until we were out of breath. My date was Doug Phillips, and he had a well-earned reputation for being a wild and enthusiastic dancer. His tuxedo dress shirt was nearly translucent with sweat; my feet ached in my high heels. The Parkside High School Class of 1997 danced and danced until midnight when the janitors flicked on the lights and kicked us out.

• • • • •

Within a few weeks, the senior class was together once again, sitting with our families as Principal Grudis opened the Senior Awards ceremony. The evening ran like a who's who among the seniors. The local Rotary, Kiwanis, Optimist, and Lions clubs offered scholarships; the Parkside PTA and National Honor Society offered awards for service and leadership. Our star student-athletes were rewarded by U.S. Marine Corp, the U.S. Army Reserves, and the National Guard. Special certificates were given to the kids in French club, Mock Trial, Business, and even one for donning the Randy the Ram costume for School Spirit. Three senior girls won recognition from Bowie State University. Name after name was called, but none of them was mine.

Until Mrs. Davis rose and headed to the podium to announce the Thomas H. Williams Old Home Prize. My heart thudded in my chest. Mrs. Davis read aloud the requirements for the prize: a senior enrolled at a Wicomico or Somerset County school, enrolled in Advanced English, with a thesis based on the Eastern Shore and its history. I had covered those bases. *Would she say my name?* There was an envelope. *Did I do enough?* She opened it. She looked up into the audience. *Please be looking for me, please be looking for me.* She paused for a second.

"Stephanie Fowler."

I swear, just for a second she found me among that sea of faces. I was jubilant! In her hands was a small, circular pewter box. Inside it was lined with blood-red, crushed velvet. My name and the prize were engraved on the lid. There was definitive proof now: I was a writer.

The last day of school found me making my familiar trek back to her classroom. She looked up, happy to see me. I was going to miss her. Terribly. I asked her if she had any spare copies of our Perrine Literature textbook. She smiled at me and dug through a stack on her desk. There was a battered one, held together with five thick strips of masking tape.

"This one," she said.

I opened the front flap and wrote: "Stephanie Fowler 1997 - On Loan From Mrs. Davis." One last hug. I didn't want to pull away. I thought of my mother and her illness. I thought of all Mrs. Davis had done for me. *Don't let go, please.*

As I walked away from her that last time, I fought back tears and tried to look ahead, to see the bright future she told me was out there, just waiting for me.

•　•　•　•　•

Incendiary

Mary Belle Parsons died on Sunday, December 22nd, 1991, leaving Casey alone in the brick rancher on Allen Road. It was a tough time for the Parsons family — their beloved matriarch was gone and left a conspicuous void in the family, especially for Casey. The sisters surrounded their father. Mary Belle would have wanted it that way.

The witticisms and wisdom of their mother continued to echo with Ellen, Barrie, and Alice, and they found themselves repeating her one-liners. "This is the biggest end of nothing," she might say when something turned out to be a disappointment; "I would rather be in Pocomoke Swamp with my back broke," she'd say when she had something to do but would rather not; and her oft summation of braggarts was "I'd like to buy him for what he's worth and sell him for what he thinks he's worth." Her Maryland Beaten Biscuits and crab cakes were passed down; her girls would forever remember that eggs, potatoes, and chicken always require salt. More than her zingers and recipes, Mary Belle's world view and her sense of order, propriety, and responsibility were the true heirlooms. Those were deeply rooted in the consciousness of each of her girls.

The loss of Mary Belle was the beginning of the de-stabilization of the Parsons nucleus. Within two years of her passing, Alice and Jess moved in with Casey. Their intention was to take care of him. After all, Casey was aging. Wouldn't it be good to have constant company and a helping hand? Casey, remaining ever faithful in his support and protection of Alice, was supportive of the idea that Jess and Alice come to live with him at the little brick rancher on Allen Road. They would take the main master bedroom while Casey would live in the little mother-in-law apartment that he and Mary Belle had added on when her mother came to live with them. Casey suggested that Jess could help with the landscaping and Alice could help with meals. It would be a mutually beneficial arrangement for all of them. Or at least, that was the plan.

For their part, Ellen and Barrie were nervous about the transition. In the years since Jess and Alice had been married, the sisters had never developed a good feeling about him. He hadn't been able to hold down a job, always bouncing from one employer to the next. He'd worked for P&A Engineering when he married Alice, but there was a growing list of failed career paths: a painter for Somerset Painters and Decorators, operator of Seals & Stripes, even the assistant superintendent of Public Works for the Town of Delmar. He'd left each of them for one reason or another. The sisters assumed it was his hot-headedness. Jess was the kind of guy who resented being told what to do because he always thought he knew more or knew a better way. That attitude made him difficult to manage and the end result was often a clash with his bosses and authority figures. When he was a maintenance mechanic at Salisbury State University, he filed a worker's compensation claim after he fell off a ladder, and in doing so, he found a new way to exit a job he didn't like.

Alice knew her sisters were always wary of Jess. Whether the sentiment was spoken outright or left as an undercurrent, Alice felt it and sometimes mentioned it to her friends. She once remarked, "Barrie just thinks I should have married a doctor." The dynamic was "haves" and "have-nots" and Jess pushed this narrative, which went largely unchallenged by Alice. The tectonic plates of their sisterhood were shifting: on one side was Alice with her husband and on the other side, Ellen and Barrie and their husbands and children. Caught in the middle was Casey. The unspoken question: was Jess — and by extension Alice — going to take advantage of their father?

When Alice and Jess moved in with Casey, the sisters begged him to charge them rent, but Casey would do no such thing. He loved all his daughters, but he knew Alice was in a different place than his oldest two. They were financially secure. Both had careers of their own as well as husbands who were making their mark in their fields. Ellen and Barrie were comfortable; Alice, on the other hand, was a teacher earning a modest salary in a rural county with a husband who was neither a hospital executive nor an insurance salesman. Alice's husband was always floundering, frequently unemployed or casting about for a side gig. Casey worried about Alice. He always had, only this time it wasn't as incidental as skinned knees from falling off her bicycle. As long as she stood by Jess, the damage was always going to be real and lifelong. He could not let his Alice struggle. *Hadn't she been through enough?*

In order to move in with Casey, Jess and Alice sold their house on Old Ocean City Road, and with the proceeds, they purchased a little cottage in Tyaskin, Maryland — a town with only a dozen or so more residents than Allen. Jess and Alice decided to rent it out. This earned them a small monthly income after they paid the mortgage on it. The responsibilities of being a landlord must have proved too much for Jess. During a visit with the Nevilles, Dawn overheard Jess say that he knew people in New Jersey who could set a fire and the best arson investigator wouldn't be able to tell the difference. Dawn thought the comment was strange, but it was followed by an even stranger tale. Jess said that the man who lived next to the cottage was stealing his electricity; Jess said he had gone by and seen an extension cord running out of the window of the cottage over to this man's house. Dawn knew Jess well enough to know that he could talk a bunch of nonsense. Not long after that, the renter moved out, which put financial pressure on Alice and Jess. Even though they had no rent to pay at Casey's house, they were hard pressed for money since Jess was working only sporadically.

And then that cottage went up in flames.

When she heard about the fire, Dawn remembered the odd remark about the New Jersey people. Her suspicions were further roused by Jess's odd behavior upon learning about the fire. A local realtor called Dawn in an effort to contact Jess because no one was sure if he knew about it. The cottage was destroyed, a total loss. Dawn finally reached Jess and told him what happened. He was stunned, utterly stricken, which made Dawn feel awful about being the bearer of such bad news for him and Alice. But then, a little later on, something happened that brought her suspicions right back to the surface. Dawn discovered that one of her sons had already told Jess about the fire before she had. His shock had been a total lie.

Was there more to the fire story than what he was letting on? Had he employed the services of those unnamed people in New Jersey? Was this arson? No one would ever know. Except, of course, Jess Davis.

But what did Alice make of the cottage fire? It must have come as a terrible surprise. There, in the remains of the fire, in the ashes and smoke, did Alice see any warning signs, any red flags to indicate the kind of danger and deception possible in the heart and mind of her husband? And if she saw or felt something ominous, did she choose to believe something else entirely? No one would ever know. Except, of course, Alice Davis.

• • • • •

A Second Chance

In 1994 on her 17th birthday, Lori Davis and a high school friend set out on a road trip from Egg Harbor, New Jersey. The destination was a small airport in Delaware. The reason for the trip: Lori was going to meet her biological father for the first time.

For her entire life, Jess Davis existed as a vague concept. She had talked to him on the phone and she had seen pictures of him, but she had no actual memories of him. One of the last times they were together was that terrifying day in 1979 when Jess took her mother's car keys and held the two of them as temporary hostages in a parking lot. The days of Jess being a father to her were lost. Gone. From the earliest time she could recall, the main figure of love and support was her mother, Nancy, a woman who was careful to never reveal the flaws in Jess's character. She held it in when he routinely failed to send child support; she kept quiet those times when she did manage to get $15 or so from him, which was not much for a single, working mother in Atlantic County, New Jersey in the early 1980s. Nothing was easy. But life took a happy turn in 1988 when Nancy met a man who was a prosecutor. He was a veritable knight in shining armor for her and Lori. Where there had once been so much apprehension and living paycheck to paycheck, they now enjoyed stability and trips to Disney World. He became Lori's father in the truest sense of the word, while Jess Davis was more like a distant uncle who called from time to time just to check in.

As a teenager, Lori decided she wanted to meet Jess. She was curious about him in the way one might be curious about seeing a museum or a national park. What would he look like? What would she learn? Her questions felt bound to the surface as there was no great longing in her heart for him. She was not a child who had built up the image of a mythical or heroic father in her mind. Quite the contrary: when she was a little girl, she used to have nightmares that he was going to kidnap her. Perhaps it was the "stranger danger" panic of the 1980s and the faces on the milk cartons at breakfast, but had Jess Davis shown up at her elementary school, she knew she would not have been able to recognize him. And so, as she grew up, Lori did not yearn for her biological father, because she had a loving paternal figure in her life. Meeting Jess was more about satisfying her own curiosity, this odd piece of her history that needed to be sorted and catalogued.

Nancy gave her blessing for the meeting. She didn't want to taint her daughter's perception of him. After all, Jess was a blank slate where Lori was concerned. Over the years, Nancy had managed to keep his impact on Lori at an absolute minimum, rendering him invisible to Lori by making him neither good nor bad. In that way, Jess was just like wallpaper — there but unnoticed.

Lori planned the road trip and Jess selected the airstrip in rural Delaware as the designated meeting spot. It was about halfway for each of them. When he approached, Lori saw a stranger. Dark hair. Blue eyes. A crooked grin. A wedding band on his left hand. Fifteen years had passed since he had last seen his daughter. In that time, Jess had created an entirely new and separate life for himself in Maryland. He had married, made friends, and had a couple of jobs. The distance was more than miles on a highway — it was deep and disconnected.

Their first meeting, despite being as awkward as one might imagine, led to a new chapter in Jess and Lori's relationship. They continued to talk on the phone and Lori finally met Alice, who had been her stepmother in name only for nearly ten years. Lori found Alice to be warm and gentle, and she appreciated how Alice welcomed her into their home whenever she came to visit. Lori saw how Alice tried to make her feel as comfortable as possible. There wasn't a trace, not a wisp, of the stereotypical evil stepmother, and for that, Lori felt very lucky.

Not long after meeting her father for the first time at that airport in Delaware, Lori met and fell in love with a young man named Johnny Lopez. They dated and it didn't take long before they knew they were right for each other. During a visit to Maryland, he proposed to her at Alice and Jess's house. Their first child, a daughter named Brianna, came in 1997, and she was followed by a sister, Serena, in 2000. By then, Lori and Jess had established a decent relationship, due in part because Alice and Lori connected so well. Alice could talk at length on any subject and then crack jokes just as fast, mirroring Lori's own sense of humor. Lori enjoyed being around her.

And there was something else. Lori sensed a yearning within Alice for this kind of relationship. Although her role as stepmother and then grandmother came late — Alice was in her early 40s — she seemed to relish it. There was room in her heart for all of them.

Early in their marriage, Alice wanted to have children with Jess and she tried to get pregnant. She began taking pre-natal vitamins and had several ob-gyn appointments. Despite her efforts, Alice was unable to get pregnant. For a woman who was so good with her nieces and nephews and who cared deeply for her students in school, it was yet another cruel circumstance of her life.

But perhaps there were other hidden reasons. Alice once lamented to Dawn that if she did get pregnant, she didn't know how she and Jess would afford private school like her sisters had done. It was a striking statement: Alice taught in the public schools of Wicomico County yet she believed they wouldn't be good enough. Or maybe she thought twice about having a child with him. During a country music festival in Allen, Jess saw a pretty woman and told Alice he was going to stick his tongue down the lady's throat. He laughed but Alice didn't. She simply drew in a deep breath and replied, "And this is why my mother doesn't want me to have children with you."

Whether it was a matter of her infertility or deciding against it financially or ultimately nixing the idea of raising a pint-sized Jess Davis, Alice faced the hard reality that, unlike her mother and sisters, she would never have a child of her own. What a crushing blow … to know that brass ring was out there, existing at the edge of her grasp, just beyond her fingertips. But just like she had with other disappointments in her life, she locked away her feelings about it, keeping them hidden behind her walls.

It might not have come as she imagined it, but with Lori and her kids, there was a second chance for Alice to have what so many other women did, and so she and Jess doted on their grandchildren. When Lori gave birth to a little boy, Johnny Lopez Jr., in 2002, they were over the moon, especially Jess. For the first time, Lori saw a different side of him. There was something light and unabashedly wholesome about Jess when he was with his grandson. He purchased little camouflage outfits and took him on outings to the Salisbury Zoo. His chest puffed out when he spoke of his grandson. It was pure and sweet. While he might not have been a good or present father to her, he blossomed in the role of grandfather.

They all saw each other once or twice a month. Lori and Johnny came down to Maryland for visits; Jess and Alice drove to New Jersey when it was their turn. In the role of grandmother, Alice called on her Allen roots as she cooked meals of fried chicken, mac and cheese, and even a roast beef dish served cold with onions. The grandkids and Lori weren't crazy about that one but Johnny loved it. Jess and Alice took their grandchildren to the boardwalk in Ocean City, and in the summer, they would get crabs and show the little ones how to crack claws. With the grandchildren, Alice wasn't reserved or defensive. The prim and proper English teacher got down on the floor and played games with them. She chased the kids around the yard with squirt guns, something quite unlike her, but she relished the moments of their laughter and how they responded to her. The little girls would play in Alice's jewelry box, rummaging through her assortment of pearls, pins, and brooches. When they tired of playing dress up, Alice would put on a Disney movie. *Lady and The Tramp* was a favorite.

For Lori, there was no question: Alice loved her grandchildren and they loved her.

·   ·   ·   ·   ·

Catalyst

In the late 1990s, Jess's old friend from Don's Bella Donna, Matthew Collier and his wife moved to North Carolina. He kept in touch with Jess and Alice and regularly came back for visits, especially for hunting trips. Matthew and Jess were part of a close knit group of men who loved to camp out for the weekend, chew the fat, and hunt. Matthew had been the one to introduce Jess to the group, and after the first outing, Jess immediately settled in as a regular member.

Often, Matthew would bring his wife and son up when he came in the fall to go deer hunting with Jess. Alice and Jess were fond of the Colliers' son, who was close in age to Lori's children. The Colliers and the Davises got along well. Matthew saw Jess, ever the cheeky rascal, settled down in a harmonious marriage. Jess often smiled at Alice and called her "buddy," a silly nickname she seemed to find endearing. The tradition of hunting trips was something that both Matthew and Jess looked forward to each year.

But all that happiness began to change, and Matthew, although living several states away, noticed Jess was heading in a bad direction. As Matthew saw it, the change began with a terrible incident. On December 4th, 2001, while working for Wicomico County, Jess came upon a guy illegally dumping deer skins. The story, according to Jess, was that he approached the man and they got into a heated argument. Jess went back to his county vehicle to get something to write down the tag number, and when he turned his back, the man pulled an axe handle from his truck and hit Jess across the neck and back. Jess filed a worker's compensation claim against Wicomico County and began receiving temporary total disability payments. He also filed for compensation for his out-of-pocket medical expenses like medications. His doctors had prescribed pain pills for Jess because of the injury as well as the subsequent surgery (to his neck and/or back). Those scripts were for opioids like oxycodone and it was a fateful introduction.

When Matthew Collier came for visits, he realized that Jess wasn't the same man. Jess had told Matthew that the incident had left him with a few fractured vertebrae in his neck, which had been fused and thus limiting his ability to turn his head. It was unfortunate: a virile man struck low in such a cowardly way.

At first, there was nothing out of the ordinary about Jess's use of the prescription pills. Jess had pain resulting from an injury and had had a serious surgery; the pain medication was both medically necessary and legitimately acquired. Jess was like any other patient, just doing what he needed to do to get through a painful and lengthy ordeal. As the months wore on, however, Jess's pain did not seem to diminish. He still required the pills. Perhaps the pain was real and Jess really did need the oxycodone. Or perhaps he just wanted it. Maybe the real answer was a mixture of actual pain and ensuing addiction as so often happens with those heavy hitting drugs.

After the incident, when Matthew and Jess went hunting, Matthew saw flashes of his old friend doing his best and functioning despite the injury, despite the pain and physical restrictions. Matthew watched as Jess forged ahead, but he knew his old friend was changed and not for the better.

•   •   •   •   •

The Impasse

Casey Parsons, always a chronicler at heart, became one of Allen's noted historians, along with George Shivers, a professor at Washington College. Starting as far back as 1971, they wrote volumes of essays and completed mountains of research, compiling interviews with town elders and writing articles about their experiences and memories of days long past in their little village. Casey and Shivers, along with a few others citizens, were the founding members of the Allen Historical Society in the late 1990s. Shivers, who literally wrote the book on Allen, was its first president while Casey served as its secretary-treasurer.

Casey was a man committed to his family and his community, and he wanted to preserve and protect the history of his home. Perhaps it was the long view of life, earned in the fiery days of war. Bearing witness to so much devastation may have spurred him to care for and maintain the ways of life around him and the home place that had always offered his soul respite. As his own sunset approached, he would often take long walks in the woods near the Wicomico Creek with his basset hound, Abigail. This ritual, this communion with nature, gave the old man great comfort. He once wrote, "In the quiet times, history whispers to us from the old mill, the church, and the stately old houses near the street." He watched as the people of the village of Allen moved about their homes, the post office, and the pond's edge, and he saw them, more clearly than ever, as players upon a stage. In his mind, he was Shakespeare crafting a play in which his neighbors unknowingly assumed their roles, sweeping in and out of a scene, act after act until twilight delivered the dark curtain of night. *Exeunt omnes.*

But living with Alice and Jess gave Casey a front row seat to a completely different drama. At home, he was witness to the dynamics of their marriage. What he observed and felt is unknowable, but one can only wonder what Casey, a man of intelligence and conscience and a man who cared for country and community, thought of Jess, a man of questionable morals whose only ambitions seemed to be of the self-serving kind. There was one moment in which Casey let his guard down during a visit from Barrie. He leaned over and whispered to her, "That man can play your sister like a fine fiddle." When Barrie pressed him for details, Casey Parsons fell silent.

His own story came to an end on Monday, July 12th, 2004, and the three sisters laid him to rest next to Mary Belle. Almost thirteen years had passed and now they would be together again, side by side in the cedar-lined cemetery in their little hometown of Allen. At the funeral, Rick Pollitt, who had walked beside Alice in Allen's Bi-Centennial parade, stood and delivered a profound and tender eulogy to a man who had inspired him as a young boy in Sunday School class. He spoke of a lifetime well spent in the service of others, of Casey's personal achievements and awards, and of a man who taught others how to die "with grace and dignity, confident in the love of a loyal family." He closed the eulogy with a quote from Shakespeare's *Romeo and Juliet* about the death of a good man adding to the luster of the stars above. Casey would have loved that, no doubt.

Whatever Casey knew of Alice and Jess, whatever his fears may have been, he took it all to the grave.

• • • • •

Just three months prior to Casey's death, there had been an epic family fight and the root of it was another worker's compensation claim. This time, Jess had filed against, Jay Ragains — the husband of Alice's niece, Kim.

Jay Ragains held the maintenance contracts for the Food Lion grocery stores on Delmarva and, in the spirit of family and trying to help Alice, he offered Jess a job as a general laborer. Kim's father, Scott Hitch, tried to warn Jay against it, telling him, "You're taking a chance on him." Jess accepted on the condition that he could take off whenever he wanted to go hunting. Jay responded by saying Jess would get paid when he worked. The arrangement was straightforward. But Scott's warning came to pass when on April 7th, 2004, Jess said he was injured while moving something heavy. One version of the story goes that he tried to prevent a shelf from falling on another man's head and in doing so hurt himself. Jess immediately filed a worker's compensation claim against Jay's company. In turn, Jay hired a private investigator to follow Jess and see if he really was hurt or not. When the case went to court, the private investigator produced video footage of Jess dragging a deer from the woods and loading it into a pickup truck. This was a powerful blow to his claims. Jess was livid.

One day during the ordeal, Jay went to work and found feces smeared all over his outbuildings and sheds. He didn't have to wonder who had done it; Jess boasted about it. But this wasn't some high school prank and his braggadocio framed the incident in a threatening tone, as if to say, *you might have won this round, but I'm still here and I can do whatever I want to you.*

The worker's compensation case lurched onward with Jess and his attorney filing issues with the court and asking for disability payments. Jess was still receiving disability payments stemming from the 2001 worker's compensation case against Wicomico County. To the family, Jess appeared to be working the system to his advantage and he never returned to work for Jay Ragains.

The anger and tension within the family over the worker's compensation issue and Jess's bizarre behavior collided with the grieving over Casey's death and the payout of his estate. The house was at the heart of the issue. Although Jess and Alice had been living in the house for more than ten years, it belonged to all three women. Casey had said he wanted the house to go to Alice and just about everyone in Alice's orbit seemed to understand that point. He wanted to ensure she was taken care of no matter what, but that wish never made it into his will, which meant that the sisters each owned a third of the house. Legally, it wasn't even a question. Barrie and Ellen decided to have the house appraised and let Alice purchase it for a third of the appraisal value. A sweetheart deal from their perspective, but to Jess and Alice, it felt like a betrayal. Prior to Casey's death, Barrie and Ellen had openly considered turning over their ownership in the house to Alice, but the idea soured over time as Jess and Alice continued to fumble financially.

From Barrie and Ellen's point of view, they saw a pattern of irresponsibility with money. They had been uncomfortable with their father constantly footing the bills for their sister and brother-in-law. Barrie had repeatedly counseled her father against letting Alice and Jess live there rent-free. She had urged him to charge Alice a little something and then put the money away in a CD or an annuity so Alice would have a little nest egg should anything happen to Casey. But Casey did none of those things. In his tenderhearted weakness for Alice, he bought the groceries despite both Alice and Jess bringing in their own incomes — Alice as a teacher and Jess receiving worker's compensation disability payments. Casey had even taken out a home equity loan and gave the money to Alice for reasons that were never clear to the sisters. Just before Casey passed away, he had instructed Barrie to sell his car and give Alice the proceeds.

Barrie and Ellen weren't sure that simply giving Alice the home would teach her anything. Wasn't it about time for Alice to be held responsible for her money? Maybe this was as good an opportunity as they could get.

The settlement of the house set an ugly tone for the months ahead. Alice acquiesced and proceeded to obtain a mortgage for the house. While Barrie and Ellen thought they were being more than fair, Alice and Jess did not see the generosity. Other family members sided with Jess and Alice, feeling that Casey's wishes weren't being completely honored, but Barrie, as the executor, was legally bound to execute the will as it was written — and Casey had never changed his will. Barrie felt she had to divide everything into thirds as evenly as possible. The fight over Casey's money continued when Barrie confronted Alice about using Casey's ATM card. She was making regular withdrawals — some as large as $1,000 — from his bank account, which prompted Barrie to confront her. "You can't do this," Barrie told her. But Alice protested, saying their father told her she could have whatever she needed.

This was more fuel for Jess's fire. In his mind, Alice's sisters were squeezing them ... *Barrie and Ellen were well off with financially successful husbands. Why did they need to do this? Why were the two older sisters taking from them, knowing full well that they were just barely getting by?* He stewed and he fumed: instead of taking care of their sister — as their father had wished — Barrie and Ellen were now saddling Alice with a mortgage. To Jess, it was all about the money.

For the two older sisters, it was all about the world versus him. No amount of logic or reason would ever sway him or calm him and they had had enough of Jess Davis. The three sisters were approaching a great impasse and it came when the estate was finally settled in full. After the funeral costs, loans, and the like, each sister received a payout of a few thousand dollars. In Jess's eyes, it was a raw deal and he was angry. Within days of getting their lump sum, Jess saw Jay Ragains at the Bagel Bakery in Salisbury. Jess was in the mood for a fight — the worker's compensation claim, the house, the money, constantly being looked down upon — and it came to the surface. Jess confronted Jay and they got into a physical altercation, which resulted in Jay filing second degree assault charges against Jess on July 20th, 2005. Then he followed that with a domestic violence protective order against Jess on August 1st, 2005.

It was all too much for Ellen who felt steeped in frustration and exasperation. Whatever her sister saw in Jess Davis, she could not, and Ellen was no longer going to tolerate any of it. Years of undertones of resentment, hurt, and suspicion were compounded by the worker's compensation debacle, the settlement of Casey's estate, the fist fight in a bagel shop parking lot, assault charges and a protective order. The lines were drawn and Ellen had to choose a side — she chose her family. The relationship between Ellen and Alice would never be the same.

The damage was to be irreversible, and the family split. To one side was Jess and Alice; the other side was her sisters and their husbands. Barrie and Ellen loved their sister, but found themselves unable to wade through the murkiness of her life and relationship with Jess Davis. The family, without Mary Belle and Casey, was splintering.

Alice was beside herself over the turmoil within her family. As was her way, she tried to keep it hidden, but the constant anxiety and rollercoaster of emotions seemed to manifest on her body. Alice developed a strange case of psoriasis and a doctor prescribed a drug called Soriatane, which she took and then suffered the side-effects. During a senior awards ceremony, Dawn Neville sat behind Alice and watched as strands of Alice's hair fell out, onto her shoulders, and then drifted to the auditorium floor.

Alice confided in Dawn about the psoriasis and the troubles within her family and Dawn was pained to see her friend so upset and even more so when she saw what the Soriatane and stress were doing to her.

Dawn also began to suspect that Alice was drinking more; her evening martini had become far more than just an evening ritual. On road trips, Alice would go through a full handle of vodka, nearly two liters, in just a few days. She could knock back her martinis at an astonishing rate. At the copier, Dawn watched as Alice's hands trembled. *Was this from nerves? Or was it related to alcohol?* Dawn suspected the latter. Another day, Alice came in with a terrible, dark bruise on her arm. Dawn asked her what had happened and

Alice's answer was chilling: "Well, if you want to know the truth, I think I had a little too much to drink, and when I came to, I was on the kitchen floor." Dawn was stunned and told Alice she needed to ease up.

All Alice could say was, "I know, I know. I just need to get it together."

Toward the end of 2005, Barrie tried to see Alice twice. The first time was to drop off some books from the Allen Historical Society. Alice did not let Barrie inside. There was no invitation to sit down or have a drink as their parents might have done with a visitor. Barrie stood in the doorway as Jess walked back and forth four or five times. Like a shark lurking on the perimeter of a coral reef, he kept his steely eyes on Barrie who felt his presence behind her sister. The encounter gave Barrie a creepy feeling, one that bordered on sinister, and as she drove away, she couldn't shake her thoughts: that Alice was going to pay for standing there and talking to her.

On Alice's 50th birthday in December 2005, Barrie bought her a pair of diamond earrings and decided to try one more time. She drove to the house and knocked on the door. Again, Alice opened the door but would not invite her inside. Barrie gave her the diamond earrings and Alice thanked her. The entire transaction took place on the threshold of the front door.

After that visit, Barrie stopped going to the old family house on Allen Road. From then on, in the years ahead, contact with Alice was minimal and limited to emails or phone calls. It was as casual as if they were old school mates or neighbors from down the road instead of sisters. And then the phone calls stopped being returned. Was Alice even getting the messages? Then emails to Alice started bouncing back. Had their internet been turned off? Once in a grocery store, Barrie asked Alice for her new email address and she offered up her Parkside email account. Although her conversations with Alice were friendly, they were superficial, revealing that the fracture between the sisters was complete.

For the Parsons sisters, there would be no healing, no making right the wrongs inflicted upon one another.

• • • • •

"But what about Alice?"

In the mid-morning hours of Tuesday, October 6th, 2009, Jess Davis called the police. Their home in Allen had been robbed, he said, and he needed to file a report.

Corporal M. Pardoe, from the Wicomico County Sheriff's Office, arrived at the home shortly before noon. Jess said he had gone for a walk around 7:30 a.m., and when he came back around 9:30 a.m., he noticed the screen on the front porch had been cut. This made him suspicious so he went inside the house and discovered they had been robbed. The list of stolen goods was impressive: six guns, two gun scopes, two trail cameras, some of his hunting clothes, a digital camera, a video camera, a Rolex watch, a pearl necklace, a Swarovski dinner ring, and sterling silver flatware. The staggering sum of the losses was just over $25,000.

As he made his report to the deputy, Jess said that just a day prior, he had seen two young black men in a strange blue Chevy pickup with Virginia plates in their neighborhood. The truck even stopped in front of his house and Jess thought maybe one of the men needed to use the bathroom. If that lead didn't pan out, well then, he was quick to offer up another possible suspect — a young woman named Jessica Pamela Cordrey.

• • • • •

How Jess met Jessica is a mystery. There are several versions of the story. In one, he met her at a doctor's office when the receptionist called out "Jess" and they both stood up. In another version, he was at Walmart and someone called "Jess Davis" to the tire center. He said he was curious about who had the same name as him so he went back to see who it was. Whatever the case, it lead to a relationship between the two and culminated in Jessica moving into the Davis home.

Like Jess, she also had a troubled background. She had been arrested twice in 2008 on drug charges. The first was in June in which she pled guilty and paid $157.50 in fines and court fees. The second arrest came in December but she was not prosecuted.

Jess told his friends and family that he was convinced this woman was his relative. He even tried convincing Lori and Johnny, she might even be a long-lost sister. He said he knew his father cheated on his mother, which made it plausible. Lori and Johnny as well as Jess's actual sister, Patricia, did not believe it. This woman was far too young and had no ties to their family at all. Lori, Johnny, and Patricia were suspicious … *what was going on?* And then their minds went to a loathsome place: was Jess having an affair right in front of Alice?

The truth was the family had been struggling since the summer of 2007 when Lori and Johnny's little boy, Johnny Jr., drowned in the pool at the Lopez home in New Jersey. The devastation and the grief were immeasurable and it crippled the entire family. It was just so inconceivable … a beautiful life taken so suddenly and tragically. Jess and Alice were utterly heartbroken for Lori and Johnny, for their grandchildren, and for themselves. Jess, in particular, took the news hard. In the months that followed, the family began working through their grief, each one in their own way. Lori was unable to go back to work. She had been working with a non-profit organization in Atlantic County helping people with disabilities. Part of her job had been to teach their clients about anger management and grief. With the loss of Johnny Jr., she found herself in an unthinkable situation: heartbroken yet with two children to care for, to nurture and love and protect. Eventually, Lori opened a day-care center in her home and then welcomed another son, Anthony, with Johnny in 2009. Working with children was a road back to herself, a path out of darkness and misery.

But Jess couldn't seem to let go of his grandson's death. He felt distant. Lori noticed that Jess didn't seem to have the same warmth about him. He was rougher and agitated. She wondered if he was abusing the pain pills. She knew he was drinking. The light she once saw in him was dimming, and it was beginning to scare her. And now she suspected he was having an affair.

For her part, Alice was relatively tight-lipped about Jessica, a complete stranger that her husband had injected into their private home life. Dawn Neville only learned about it when Bobbi McCabe, a woman who cleaned houses for both the Nevilles and the Davises, asked Dawn if she knew the young woman who was living with Alice and Jess. Dawn was shocked and didn't know who she was talking about. Bobbi told her the woman was a cousin of Jess's, but both Bobbi and Dawn were suspicious of the relationship. Cindy Bennett got a different version of events: Jess had given Alice a sad story about Jessica being a relative in need of their help and that the loss of Johnny Jr. made him want to reach out and be a support for her. Alice didn't like it and didn't want her there, but seemed to feel she had no choice in the matter. It sounded to Cindy that Jess was leaning on Alice's grief over Johnny Jr. as well as Alice's soft spot for helping others in order to cover up something more nefarious.

By June 17th, 2009, Alice had had enough of the situation:

she filed a motion with the District Court in Wicomico County to have her evicted from the home, and by July 8th, 2009, Jessica Pamela Cordrey was gone.

Three months later, on that October morning as he stood in front of the police, Jess named her as a possible burglary suspect.

• • • • •

Corporal Pardoe turned the case over to Maryland State Police Trooper First Class Sabrina Metzger. While she spoke with Jess, a crime scene tech dusted the house for fingerprints and took photographs. Metzger felt something was odd about Jess's story, but she pursued the offered leads. She went house to house in Allen, interviewing the neighbors to see if they saw or heard anything that morning or if they had any recollection of two young black men or a dark blue pickup with out-of-state tags. No one had seen or heard anything.

Metzger thought Jess's story was as odd as he was, and she suspected he had staged the entire event, especially when not a single one of the items reportedly taken turned up at local pawn shops. The problem was that there wasn't any direct proof that Jess was involved. Metzger went to Parkside High School to interview Alice. The conversation did not yield anything of value, except it did leave Metzger with a lasting impression of his wife as a nice, poised, and intelligent woman. Just what one might expect from a seasoned English teacher. Metzger walked away, wondering to herself, *how are these two people together ... they don't fit. This smart lady is married to that guy?!*

Soon afterward, Alice told Dawn that Jess had interrupted the burglary. He told her that he pulled up in the driveway and saw a strange truck. Jess realized it was a daytime break-in. He chased the two men off as best he could, but they were able to get away with some of their valuables. She was thankful the intruders had not hurt her cats. She lamented the loss of her grandmother's dinner ring. She felt violated, she said.

The fingerprint analysis did not reveal anything unusual or out of the ordinary, which effectively cancelled out the theory of the young black men in a phantom pickup truck. The lead regarding Jessica Cordrey, who Jess told police was his cousin, also hit a dead end. There was no evidence, physical or otherwise to suggest her involvement, or the involvement of any other unknown individual. The items were taken from all over the home — from bedrooms to the basement — which suggested the "burglar" would have to have known exactly where those items were. Metzger's investigation did not uncover a single lead that pointed to a possible suspect other than Jess Davis himself, but her suspicions were all she had.

With a police report in hand, Jess filed a claim with their homeowner's insurance for $25,000, which State Farm paid. The investigation remained open and unsolved. Even though members of law enforcement suspected that Jess Davis had staged the crime and committed insurance fraud, without hard evidence pointing directly at him, there was little they could do about it.

Jess had good reason to need that money. He was going to be a father again.

He had met a young woman from the Dominican Republic by the name of Yangeri Esquea. She was half his age, good-looking, and receptive to his advances. How he met her is unknown, but she was cleaning houses. Although Alice was able to remove Jessica from their lives, she would not be able to do the same with Yangeri. Jess was a man consumed. The affair was hot and heavy, and Yangeri got pregnant. This changed things for him. Jess began planning an ex-pat life with her, away from Alice and Lori and his grandchildren.

• • • • •

On the night of Sunday, February 7th, 2010, as Lori and Johnny were preparing for their Super Bowl party, Jess called Lori to tell her his good news: he had a girlfriend and she was pregnant with twins. He was elated at this new chapter in his life.

Lori stood amid the food trays and party plates with her mouth agape. She was stunned. *What on earth was he talking about? Who was this woman? Twins?* As Lori tried to get her bearings, tried to make sense of this inconceivable information in front of her, she began to cry. The news made her feel sick to her stomach and her mind immediately went to Alice.

"But what about Alice?"

Jess replied that she knew and was happy for them.

That didn't make any sense at all.

And then there was a shift. Jess realized Lori was crying and upset. She wasn't happy for him or Yangeri or the babies; she was asking about Alice and her reaction to the news. When Jess began to sense this, he turned on her. He began berating her, tearing her down for not supporting him and his new family — *her new siblings.*

Finally, Johnny intervened on the phone call. He couldn't let Jess do this to her. What kind of father does that to his daughter anyway? No, this was going to end. He told Jess that Lori was done with him for the night.

Jess flew hot at Johnny and began screaming and cursing. Johnny would not budge. As far as he was concerned, the conversation was over. And then Jess began to threaten Johnny. No one was going to tell him what to do. No one.

And with that, the line went dead.

•   •   •   •   •

The relationship between Lori and Jess was never the same after that conversation on Super Bowl Sunday. Subsequent conversations devolved into threats against her husband. Lori was scared; Johnny began carrying a gun. When they were home, they would watch cars passing by their front windows, hoping it wasn't Jess. Because of his increasingly erratic and threatening behavior, Lori barred Jess from family activities. He was no longer welcome at their home or around her children, but Alice was still welcome. No matter what Jess did, he could not change how Lori felt about Alice.

And so Alice made her trips to New Jersey alone. It was during one of these visits when Lori sat down with Alice on their front step. Alice told her Jess was down in the Dominican Republic, and the two women talked about the girlfriend and the babies. Lori was heartbroken as she listened to Alice make excuses for Jess and the affair, but little could have prepared her for what Alice said next. She was going to help raise Jess's babies.

Oh Alice... what are you thinking? Lori could not believe it. Was this a result Alice's own desire for children or was this something more desperate? Was this an attempt to keep Jess at all costs? Lori begged Alice to think it over. The very notion of Alice having to raise the children who were the product of an affair when she couldn't bear her own made Lori sick. Alice, in her quiet way, insisted she could make it all work. Lori was watching her father destroy everything that mattered in his life. He was an unpredictable wrecking ball, swinging wildly and devastating his relationships with his wife, his daughter, his son-in-law, and his grandchildren.

Nothing more came of the pregnancy, however. As Lori understood it, not long after Alice had said she would help raise the babies, the young woman had a miscarriage.

Lori wanted to help Alice. She told her that she could come live with her and Johnny and the kids. Even Patricia, his sister, offered to let Alice come stay. Alice politely declined their offers, saying it wouldn't work. "He'd know where to find me. Besides, Jess would never hurt a hair on my head."

And that was all she had to say.

• • • • • •

"If anything ever happens to me..."

Around the time of Casey Parson's death and the family quarrels, there was an unusual exchange at Parkside between Dawn and Alice. It happened unexpectedly, like a lightning strike on a clear blue day. Alice grabbed Dawn's arm and said, "If anything ever happens to me, promise me you'll look after my cats and Lori. My sisters won't be as kind to her as you will be. Promise me."

Startled by the suddenness of this ominous request, Dawn promised ... yet she couldn't help but think, *what is this all about?*

On another occasion, Dawn saw Alice looking downcast and asked her what was wrong. Alice replied, "My life is in the toilet."

"Alice, your life is not that bad!" Dawn said, trying to be light hearted and make her friend feel better.

"Oh yes, it is," she said. "You just don't know."

This was a hard and revealing moment of truth for Alice. Her life was messy, a chaotic whirlwind of secrets and betrayal and it was beyond anything she could control. The little brick rancher on Allen Road, once home to a prosperous, well-adjusted middle class family, was now occupied by an unhappy middle-aged couple who weren't even sharing the same bedroom anymore. Alice had the master bedroom while Jess was living in the little apartment where

Casey lived until his death. Alice buried herself in teaching and martinis while Jess, still taking pain pills and collecting disability checks from his two worker's compensation injuries, had created a side gig — running a taxidermy shop out of their house.

He had been an avid hunter for most of his life and taxidermy seemed like a good fit. He wasn't squeamish around dead animals and he could work at his pace on his own schedule right from home. Jess named his business Field of Dreams Taxidermy. But even the taxidermy business was fraught with deceit. Jess had a reputation of accepting jobs and taking deposits but not completing the work. A few of his customers even complained directly to Wicomico County Sheriff Mike Lewis, who could only suggest they take it up with Jess in civil court. Mike Lewis knew Jess Davis. His family had hunted with Jess over the years and his father and brothers had a few trophies mounted by Jess. While Mike could understand the frustration, a dispute over a dead deer head wasn't a criminal matter.

And to add insult to Alice's injury, Jess had Yangeri working in his taxidermy shop, cleaning, answering phones, and doing filing work. This was on the heels of Alice having to evict Jessica Corddrey from the home. At every step, the other women in his life were right there, on her property, in her home, in his bed. Alice could not escape it, and her pride would not allow her to admit she had chosen poorly. Alice would not allow her sisters an "I told you so" moment. Financially, she was anchored to him. Alice was in deep and the water level was only rising.

Her mother was gone. Her father was gone. She was estranged from her sisters, brothers-in-law, nieces, and nephews. Jess was all she had left. The only bright side was Lori and the grandchildren. Without them, she would have been completely isolated, and even then, Jess was doing his damnedest to push them away.

Yet some of the distance was of Alice's own making. Dawn Neville felt Alice pulling away shortly after the death of Casey and the ensuing fallout with Barrie and Ellen. Jess was making it hard for Alice to maintain normal friendships. He was flaunting his affairs to the husbands of her friends, like the time he passed his cell phone around at a party to show Bill Neville and a few other men pictures he had taken of Yangeri in lingerie, posed on Alice's bed. Once, at a dinner party at the Nevilles home, Jess shoved a cell phone down his pants and took a picture of his genitals right there in the middle of the living room. Alice immediately grabbed the phone and deleted the photo. After that, Dawn and Bill stopped inviting Jess and Alice to parties, preferring instead to opt for dinner when it would be just the four of them. But then, Alice started to decline the invitations even when Dawn practically begged her to come over. Alice wouldn't even go to lunch with her anymore. It was an affirmation of Dawn's suspicion that Alice was unhappy, struggling with her life and with Jess.

There was another problem as Dawn saw it: Jess's growing dependence on pain pills, which appeared to border on addiction. His regular use of oxycodone was common knowledge; everyone knew about his injury and the resulting surgery. But that wasn't all. Once, Alice confided in Dawn that she had found the remains of a burned out marijuana joint in the ashtray of her car. Jess also continued to drink, sometimes heavily. Dawn often wondered if some of their financial troubles stemmed from both Jess's drug use and their combined alcohol use.

Whether Alice admitted it to herself or not, there was a stark contrast between the life she wanted to build with Jess Davis and the life she actually had with Jess Davis. Walking down the aisle at her wedding, she must have been thinking about what could be, the world she could create for herself and Jess. She had time and he was there; as rough around the edges as he was, she could smooth that out. Certainly she could will it into existence. But Jess's untameable nature, a quality that had once been so alluring to her, now revealed itself for what it was — a fickle wildness. He had always done exactly what he wanted to do and that much would never change. Her folly was to think that he would have considered her more, that he would have been different when it came to her.

It was her undoing.

• • • • • •

"I looked into the eyes of the Devil."

Marisa Carey, and her partner, Maria, had been getting ready for the veterinarian's visit at their home in Allen. They owned several dogs and cats, and to make things easier on themselves, they paid for two house calls a year. It was spring of 2011, but Marisa felt an unusual chill in the air as she walked out to her driveway and greeted the vet. As he was getting his things from his vehicle, Marisa saw another car pulling into their driveway. Her heart sank with frustration. It was their neighbor, Jess Davis. Marisa and Maria adored his wife, Alice, but felt Jess was always more of a headache than he was helpful. She didn't need him getting into the mix of their busy day.

As Jess approached, Marisa saw that he had a packet of flyers in his hands. He handed her one and said he was sealing driveways and he would be happy to do theirs as well as the driveway at Marisa's chiropractic office. Marisa looked down at the flyer in her hands and felt a familiar pang of irritation. Between the vet's visit and trying to wrangle the dogs and cats, Marisa was frazzled and decided to brush him off. "Jess, just give me an estimate and I'll let you know."

On his way to his car, he tried another line, this time with Maria. His girlfriend, Yangeri, would clean their house wearing a thong, to which the vet joked back that maybe he needed Jess's cleaning lady.

After Jess left, Maria repeated the thong line to Marisa, which infuriated her because it harkened back to an ugly moment in 2000, not long after Marisa and Maria had moved into their home just down the street from the Davises. On that particular day, while Marisa and Jess were standing in the yard, chatting away as neighbors often do, he said, "I have something funny to tell you." And he proceeded to tell Marisa explicit details of a recent sexual encounter he had had with Alice. In the most vulgar of terms and descriptions, Jess boasted about this deeply intimate moment between two lovers, a moment in which Alice let her guard down to appease him and he took advantage.

Marisa, stunned and disgusted, snapped at him, "Jess! That's very inappropriate!"

Jess immediately cowed, realizing Marisa was angered by the story. He stammered, "Oh! Well ... well, I just thought it was funny."

The episode left Marisa with her stomach churning and her heart broken for Alice. Marisa thought to herself, *why would he tell me such a thing? We don't even know each other that well.* Marisa felt embarrassed for Alice, that her husband would tell a near stranger this incredibly private story, especially one in which his wife was so exposed. *And that he laughed about it ... he laughed about Alice's vulnerability.* It bothered Marisa, but it would not be the last thing he would do that would haunt her.

A few days after the veterinarian's home visit, Marisa left her yoga class and started to head home. But something told her not to go home just yet. Instead, she drove to her chiropractic office and saw Jess there with three Hispanic men, getting ready to offload driveway sealing equipment and tools.

"Whoa, whoa, whoa! Jess! What are you doing?"

He sauntered over to Marisa and began to hustle her. "I'm here and I'm gonna take care of you. And that guttering over there is kinda leaning over so I'll take care of that too."

Marisa stood firm. "We already discussed this. I told you to give me an estimate and I'd think about it. I did not give you the OK."

Jess took a few steps closer to her. The diminishing distance between them began to make her feel uncomfortable. "Come on now, you know me. I'm good. I'll take care of you. I'll give you a good deal. Just let me do the work." And with that, he turned to walk away from her.

"I said no."

Jess turned back around.

"You are not doing this today. I start seeing patients at 1 o'clock. You can't be sealing the driveway. The answer is no."

He turned on the charm. He pushed the hustle. He would not hear Marisa's "no."

She had had enough. "Jess, get the fuck off my property now!"

Oh, but Jess heard that. In an instant, he closed the gap between them, pushing his body forward so that he was eye to eye with her. Marisa began to panic as she watched his face turn red. His bright blue eyes went black, as if the pupils had gathered up the irises. He was inescapable now. She looked over his shoulder at the three men who had come with Jess. None of them would make eye contact with her. Her office manager was inside the building. *If I scream, would she hear me? What is he going to do to me? Is he going to hit me?*

The seconds seemed to slow for Marisa as Jess stared her down. Scenarios ran through her mind. With his face so close to hers, she was unnerved by how this violent change had come over him. It was as if someone pulled a shade down on a window, obliterating the sun from view. His eyes terrified her and she knew instinctively: *he wants to hurt me.*

It was Marisa who broke the silence first. "Jess, you need to leave now."

And just as suddenly as the shade had been drawn down, it lifted up. Jess took a step backwards and the darkness dissipated from his eyes and the paleness returned to his cheeks. He took another step back. "I'm sorry. I'm sorry." He began apologizing over and over. The maelstrom dissipated into the morning air.

Marisa waited until Jess and the other men left before she walked into her building. Her office manager took one look at her and asked what had happened. Marisa relayed the story to her, and when Maria got to the office, she repeated the story again. Both women were unsettled but relieved it was over.

Until the phone rang. It was Jess. He wanted to apologize again. But Marisa wasn't going to let him off so easily. Maybe it was a post-adrenaline rush or maybe it was having a few moments to digest what had occurred between them or maybe she was just angry, but either way, she hammered back at him.

Jess kept trying to apologize. Marisa made a stand, almost as much for Alice as for herself. Jess had scared the hell out of her. She thought, *what was he like to Alice?* The phone call ended with both Jess and Marisa agreeing to let the incident go without any further conversation. They'd just drop it.

A few days later, Maria and Marisa passed Alice and Jess on the highway. They all waved to each other. Marisa never told Alice about any of it because she didn't want to hurt her, but she wondered if Jess had. The evidence? Flowers were delivered to Marisa but they came with no note, no sender information.

Was that Alice making up for what Jess had done to her? Marisa suspected so.

• • • • •

In the summer of 2011, Alice came for a surprise visit at their home. Marisa and Maria were happy to see her. Alice was unusually upbeat and she had good reason: she was selling their house and moving to an apartment in Canal Woods in Salisbury. There was a genuine spark to Alice, a light in her eyes that they hadn't seen in a long time. As the women spoke, the subject of whether or not Jess was moving with her did not come up, but both Marisa and Maria got the impression this was *her move*. She wanted to go and they didn't blame her. They knew about the girlfriend from the Dominican Republic and they felt sure Alice knew about her too. As they saw it, Alice deserved better than Jess Davis and his bullshit.

And there was one more thing. Marisa had recently teased Alice for wearing a pair of worn out shoes. Marisa and Maria, and most of the neighbors, knew the Davises were constantly having financial difficulties; Jess was always hustling someone for a job or asking to borrow money. But still, Marisa hated to see Alice walking around in ragged, dirty shoes. So, when she stopped by, she lifted her leg to show Marisa that she had purchased new shoes — a pair of Faded Glory canvas slip ons.

Marisa and Maria were proud of her. The big move. The new shoes. Alice was beaming. Was that a glimmer of happiness in her eyes? The visit had a hint of a fresh beginning and it left Marisa and Maria feeling optimistic for Alice. And yet, not long after that moment, their hopes would be extinguished and replaced with an unimaginable fear.

Part III

"By the pricking of my thumbs, something wicked this way comes."

MACBETH
ACT IV, SCENE i

"Have you seen the news?"

It was an ordinary Tuesday, the morning after the Labor Day holiday in September of 2011. While I was settling into my office at Lifestar Ambulance, a private ambulance company owned and operated by my mother, I overheard the two women across the hall in our medical billing office talking about a teacher from Parkside High School who was missing. Although my ears perked at the mention of my high school, I dismissed it. More than 14 years had passed since I had graduated, which made me certain that the missing person wouldn't be anyone I remembered because I was sure most of my teachers would have retired or moved on.

A few minutes after 8:00 a.m., my phone rang. It was my sister, Kristen.

"Steph, have you seen the news?" Her voice had a high, sharp edge to it. I sensed urgency in her tone, like the time my mother called to tell me a plane had hit a building in New York City. *Something awful must be happening.*

"No, not yet. Why? What's up?"

"Mrs. Davis is missing."

"What?" I didn't understand. My mind began to reel as I frantically pulled up the local news on my computer. A chilling panic crept into the room and slid up my spine.

Something was wrong and I knew it. Down into my bones. She was the kind of teacher that we could set our watches by. Her disappearance made no sense. How does a woman like Alice Davis just go missing?

The initial details sounded like a kidnapping. I logged into Facebook and read the headlines: "Search For Missing Wicomico County Teacher." I devoured the available details, which were few and bizarre. Her husband had reported her disappearance on

Sunday evening after she failed to return home from a shopping trip to the Walmart in Fruitland, Maryland. The police discovered her blue Honda Fit in the Big Lots shopping center directly across the Route 13 highway. She was last seen wearing blue shorts and a yellow t-shirt. The missing person report noted that she was 5'10" and 185 pounds with brown hair and blue eyes. The reporters and police agencies asked anyone with any information to come forward.

Accompanying each article was the picture from her Maryland driver's license. Her blue eyes stared back at me from the computer screen. There was no mistake — it was her. *But how could she be gone?* Suddenly every awful emotion I'd ever felt in her classroom was with me again. In full bloom. Shock and fear. The unknown. But this time was different. This time the energy was dark and malevolent in a way that illness can not manifest.

I read the articles again and again. My mind raced ...

This is all wrong.

•　•　•　•　•

Case File #11-003437

At 7:34 p.m. on Sunday, September 4ᵗʰ of the Labor Day Weekend in 2011, Deputy First Class Dennis Taylor from the Wicomico County Sheriff's Department responded to 3574 Allen Road for a 911 call regarding a missing person. Taylor arrived at the small brick rancher and met with the caller, Jess Davis, who said his wife was missing. Almost immediately, the deputy noticed that Jess was intoxicated. Something didn't feel right.

As Deputy Taylor began to ask questions, Jess started to tell a disoriented and rambling story: he had given her $700 in cash and sent her to the Fruitland Walmart to buy clothes, but first she was going to stop by the home of her friend, Mary Starnes. He said Alice had drank between three and five vodka martinis before leaving home at 6:30 p.m. She hadn't returned and that caused him to worry. "She's never gone this long," he said.

One could only imagine Deputy Taylor thinking: *so your wife goes to visit a friend and then to Walmart to shop, but you call us an hour after she left? And you let her drive away under the influence of three to five martinis?* The timeline made no sense at all. The whole story was a red flag.

Based on what Jess had told him, Deputy Taylor contacted the Fruitland Police Department to ask for assistance in looking for Alice, starting at the Walmart.

• • • • •

Fruitland, Maryland is an easy ten-minute drive from the Davis home, heading north on Route 13. Compared to Allen, Fruitland is a metropolis and the first signs of urban life in a predominately farming community. McDonald's and Ruby Tuesday sit at the entrance to the Walmart complex. Just to the south, a Hampton Inn hotel occupies what once was a farm field. Hunan Palace, one of Alice's favorite restaurants, is directly west of Walmart and in the same shopping center as the Big Lots store. The Wine Rack, a gas station proffering a large selection of wines, sits at an angle on the opposite corner. Car lots, apartment buildings, even a large regional sporting complex with an indoor skating rink provide just as much to the backdrop as the utility poles and traffic lights, the shade trees in the median, and the cornfields off in the distance. Fruitland is a town thriving enough to maintain a fire department with both paid and volunteer staff. The police department comprises 20 sworn officers.

The Fruitland Police Department responded to Deputy Taylor's call for help. Officers began searching Walmart and surrounding shopping centers on that stretch of Route 13, and in doing so they discovered Alice's car. It was abandoned and unoccupied in a large parking lot near the Big Lots, across the busy highway from Walmart. When they found the car, there was no blood or broken glass, nothing to indicate there had been an obvious struggle.

They contacted Deputy Taylor who was still at the Davis residence where he had been attempting to contact Alice's friend, Mary Starnes. The Fruitland Police told Taylor they'd found the car, apparently abandoned. Taylor turned his focus to Jess, telling him the calls to Mary Starnes were going directly to voicemail and, more importantly, that Alice's car had been found in the Big Lots shopping center. Jess Davis only remarked that he found it all quite strange.

That was an understatement.

Deputy Taylor left the Davis residence and headed to Fruitland to see the car. Then he went to the Sheriff's Department where he entered Alice into the National Crime Information Center, a central database maintained by the FBI. Alice Davis was filed under "Missing Persons" and the primary criteria for entry is "reasonable concern for an individual's safety."

It was getting close to midnight and there was no trace of Alice. They were losing time. With little else to go on, Deputy Taylor went back to the Davis residence.

This time, Jess was even more visibly intoxicated, but he invited the deputy inside and offered to show him where he slept. This was something Jess had not done on the first visit. Taylor looked around the bedroom and quickly surmised this was not a bedroom shared by a husband and wife. This was Jess's bedroom, but there was a purse on his bed.

"Is this Alice's?" asked Deputy Taylor.

"Yes. Go ahead and look through it."

The deputy looked at the purse and did the quick mental math. *So your wife went shopping and left her purse? She didn't turn around and come back for it and you're just now telling me?* Taylor looked through Alice's purse and found her wallet. Inside was her driver's license. The scene felt wrong. Something was up. Taylor recognized the situation was evolving and stepped out to call his superiors. He requested his backup to come quickly because he could feel the tension beginning to build between Jess and himself. When Taylor walked back into the bedroom, he noticed that Jess had removed her wallet and taken her driver's license and a few other cards. *What was he doing?*

Taylor sensed the eroding civility, but remained composed in front of Jess. He reassured Jess that he was only there to help find his missing wife. Wasn't that the whole point? But Jess was getting agitated, repeating over and over that he just wanted to go to bed.

Corporal Jeff Melvin arrived as Taylor's backup. As they began to discuss the emerging details of the case, Jess moved within a few inches of them and became confrontational: "I'm going to listen to everything you guys say. It is my right to hear what you are saying about me!"

They tried to calm him down, but his hostility persisted. Corporal Melvin saw Jess's eyes were red and glassy. They tried to ask a few more questions and continued to remind him that they were there to help find his missing wife, but Jess became enraged. "I know what you guys are trying to do!"

In an effort to defuse the stressful situation, Corporal Melvin and Deputy Taylor excused themselves and stepped just outside the front door to talk privately. Jess seized the opportunity; he slammed the door in their faces and turned off the porch light.

Although Jess Davis may have been done with the police, they were just getting started with him.

•   •   •   •   •

At about 1:30 a.m., Sergeant Kelly Matthews searched through the police databases, looking for previous reports or logs of activity for the Davis residence. He found a "Check Welfare" entry dated a year and a half prior on April 7ᵗʰ, 2010. The caller had been Lori Lopez.

On that night — two months after the terrible blowout on Super Bowl Sunday — Lori had been talking on the phone with Alice and she could hear Jess in the background, screaming a tirade of frightening threats. He said he was going to drive to New Jersey and kill Johnny. He had all he needed: guns, a car, and time. Lori was terrified. Was this the ugly side of the man her own mother had known all those years ago? Lori feared for Alice. She feared for her own safety and that of her family. She hung up the phone with Alice and immediately called the police and reported what had just happened. When the sheriff's deputy arrived at the Davis residence, Alice met with him and assured him everything was fine. Alice denied the threats and made some excuse about Lori and Jess not getting along. Jess did not appear intoxicated to the officer so he chalked it up to family issues and cleared the call. Nothing more came of it.

Lori Lopez told Sergeant Matthews that her father was crazy. And when he asked her if she thought Jess could be involved with Alice's disappearance, Lori did not hesitate: "Absolutely."

The next phone call Sergeant Matthews made was to Jess's sister, Patricia Slocum. She said Jess had called her shortly after Alice failed to return home from Walmart. In addition to the extramarital affair, the pregnancy, and miscarriage, Patricia said her brother had a problem with alcohol. Patricia also expressed concern that Alice wouldn't leave Jess, that she loved him too much and wouldn't have left behind her cats. And Patricia revealed one last chilling detail: her brother had become increasingly delusional.

At about 3:00 a.m., Sergeant Matthews met a few other officers at the parking lot where Alice's car had been discovered. They began to inspect the car in closer detail. There was fresh grass in the undercarriage. Inside the vehicle, they found Jess's wallet with his driver's license in the pocket of the driver's side door as well as an unknown white substance on the fabric of the rear fold-down seats. But more importantly, they found brown hair on the floor panel of the rear compartment of the trunk on the driver's side. The color and length appeared consistent with Alice's. The police had her driver's license photo for comparison. The thickness of the clump of hair was about the size of a pencil.

An hour later, Sergeant Matthews went to their home. He knocked on the door and announced his presence, but Jess never appeared. As he walked around the house, he noticed an orange bottle of oxy cleaner outside near the back door.

Red flags. Everywhere.

Nothing the police were uncovering did anything to assuage their concerns. They had a cheating husband who had made death threats against his own daughter's husband. Add in alcohol. Take into account his bizarre behavior. Fresh grass. Brown hair. Each new detail only reinforced a need for the spotlight to be aimed as brightly and as directly as possible at Jess Henry Davis, Jr.

•   •   •   •   •

"Jess knows more than he's telling us."

That Sunday evening, two things were happening almost simultaneously: the police had started their investigation into Alice's disappearance and Jess was reaching out to Alice's closest friends to ask if they had seen or heard from her. Of course no one had. Just before he called 911, he had placed multiple calls to Mary Starnes as well as his own sister. Then he dialed her friends, including Anne Collins, Cindy Bennett, and Dawn Neville. There were no phone calls to Lori or Alice's sisters. Instead, he chose to call her friends. If he was trying to elicit sympathy, all he managed to do was raise their suspicions.

Anne Collins immediately knew something bad had happened. As she listened to Jess recount his story, she realized the puzzle pieces weren't fitting together. He was in a fever, talking fast and bouncing from one detail to another, letting loose a wild and illogical stream of consciousness. Anne knew they didn't have $700 for Alice to go shopping; just a few weeks prior, Jess had borrowed $300 from her, which he had managed to pay back. They never had that kind of spare money. And she knew Alice wasn't likely to leave the house late on a Sunday afternoon. Anne was unnerved, especially when Jess began to offer up suggestions as to what might have happened, saying things like "Could someone have knocked her in the head and kidnapped her?" It sounded to Anne like he was trying out different theories to see what might sound best, most plausible. It sounded phony. It sounded like Jess had done something terrible.

Anne, ever the pragmatist, gave him her best advice: "Be honest and straightforward with the police. You cannot try to equivocate.

You have to tell them everything you know because they will find out and it's worse if you lie to them."

Within seconds of her stern warning, Jess ended the call. As she put the phone down, a chilling thought ran through Anne's mind: *if he's done something to Alice, what else could he do? He knows where I live.*

He tried his story again with Cindy Bennett. When she answered the phone, he blurted out, "Do you know where Alice is?" Cindy was caught off guard. Although they were friends, Cindy and Alice weren't so close as to know each other's schedules. He launched into his story again, but this time, he began to add another layer, saying "I just don't know what to do without her. We've been together for so long."

Cindy didn't understand any of it. Jess sounded like he was crying. She told him she would let him know if she heard from Alice. She said she would pray about it. His response: "If something has happened to her, I don't know what I'll do."

When Cindy hung up, she replayed the conversation over in her mind. *If Alice went to the store, then why is he calling me from her cell phone? Wouldn't she have taken that with her? And it's only been a few hours so why is he calling me?* Everything about the phone call felt weird to Cindy; it made her wonder if things between Jess and Alice had gotten so bad that she had finally left him. But she quickly canceled that idea because the school year had just started. Alice was too conscientious to shirk her teaching duties. She wouldn't just walk away from her career. And the cats. Alice would never have abandoned them either.

All night, she replayed the conversation in her mind and decided she would contact Alice's sister, Barrie, in the morning.

Dawn Neville was in Big Bend, Oregon visiting her son, daughter-in-law, and grandchild. They were having a good time at a family afternoon cookout when Dawn's phone rang. She looked at the caller ID and was happy to see that it was Alice. She answered the phone in an excited exclamation, "Alice Davis! What are you doing calling me out here?!"

"Oh Dawn, this is Jess." He sounded normal. "I'm sorry to bother you. I forgot you all were out in Oregon. I'm so sorry to bother you."

Dawn told him it was alright.

And then, Jess started to cry, or what sounded to Dawn like he was trying to cry. "Alice is missing and I can't find her. I don't know what to do."

Dawn was stunned, but told Jess to calm down and give her the details. Jess gave her the story about how he had given Alice $700 to go shopping, that it was the money he got from selling his truck and she had been gone two hours. He said he didn't know what was going on. Dawn tried to reason with him that two hours wasn't a long time for a woman to go shopping. Jess was insistent that something was wrong because her watch and rings were on the table next to the sofa. He said he had called the police.

"You called the police?" Dawn was incredulous. Her mind was trying to make sense of it all. She *knew* Alice. Going shopping late on a Sunday afternoon doesn't sound like her. Alice would be making a cocktail, not preparing to go to Walmart, especially on a holiday weekend.

Even Dawn's husband, Bill, tried talking to Jess, but none of it sounded right. Jess just kept saying that she'd gone missing and he didn't know where she was. The Nevilles couldn't do anything from Oregon except wait and see what the next day would bring. Maybe Alice just needed some time alone and would return soon. Dawn and Bill recalled the last time they saw Jess and Alice: it was a few days before they left for Big Bend. Bill wanted to return a steam cleaner he had borrowed. Jess and Alice were sitting in the front yard by a little fish pond, having martinis when the Nevilles pulled up. They offered the Nevilles a couple of martinis and even talked about selling the house.

Dawn knew the lady who owned the condo in Canal Woods that Jess and Alice had been looking at. She told Dawn about Jess and Alice coming to see the unit and how they sat close together on her sofa and how he kept his hands on Alice the entire time. The lady and the Davises came to an agreement: she would take her condo off the market until they could sell their house.

During that last encounter with Jess and Alice, everything seemed fine to Dawn and Bill. There wasn't a hint of tension between them, nothing to suggest a life-changing calamity was mere days away.

The next morning was Labor Day, and it brought darker news to Big Bend. A detective called Dawn and wanted to know if Alice had access to the Nevilles' house. Dawn told the detective she did — Alice had a key and knew the garage code. Bill and Dawn granted permission for them to search. The fact that a detective was on the line was sobering and filled Dawn with foreboding. It meant that thought of Alice running off for a bit of solitude was gone. Instead, Dawn began to fear the worst. She suspected Jess knew more than he was telling. What if Jess owed a drug dealer? Had he sent Alice with $700 to pay a debt and something terrible happened to her? Bill's own thoughts aligned with Dawn's. He also thought drugs were involved and that Alice's disappearance was a kidnapping.

When Mary Starnes called Dawn, she was crying hysterically and said that Jess had just been to her house. Mary told Dawn how distraught Jess was and that she just felt terrible for him. This prompted a warning from Dawn: "I want you to be very cautious about him, Mary. Be cautious about how much access he has to you and your home." What Dawn did not tell Mary Starnes: *something is very wrong here and Jess knows more than he's telling us.*

• • • • •

On that Monday morning, Cindy made good on her promise to herself and reached out to Barrie. Cindy and Don Bennett were friendly with the Tilghmans because, in addition to being connected by Alice, they all attended the same church. Barrie had even been Cindy's Sunday School teacher, a tradition that harkened back to Casey's influence.

Labor Day morning found Barrie preoccupied: they had company and she was babysitting her grandchildren, not to mention she was keeping an eye on their two new kittens, Ike and Mamie, named after the Eisenhowers. When Cindy got Barrie on the line, she told her that Jess had called the previous evening to tell her that Alice was missing. He was frantic, Cindy said.

"Missing?!" Barrie was somewhere between shock and disbelief.

A strange sensation came over her as she listened to Cindy recount the story Jess had given her, that Alice had vanished while she was shopping at the Fruitland Walmart. *What was going on?*

Barrie's mind was spinning. Finally, she spoke: "Well, either she's gotten fed up and thankfully left the son of a bitch or he's done something to her."

After Barrie hung up the phone, she sat for a moment. The last communication she had had with Alice was an email at the end of August, just about a week or so prior, in which she told Barrie that she and Jess intended to sell the house and move into an apartment in Canal Woods. Jess would be able to fish in the creek there, she wrote, and if she or Ellen wanted the house back then they could have first refusal. Jess and Alice had been having yard sales and were selling off much of the furniture Mary Belle and Casey had acquired. Barrie spoke of the email and Alice's plans with Ellen. It seemed like their sister was about to embark on a whole new strange chapter of her life with Jess and neither Barrie nor Ellen quite knew what to make of it: Alice leaving her childhood home, selling off their parents' belongings, and Jess Davis fishing in a dark creek just down the road from the Walmart in Fruitland.

For Barrie, Alice was too much like their mother. Those two women would no sooner go to Walmart on a Sunday afternoon than they would fly to the moon. No, Mary Belle would always shop during the day so she could be home in the evening, likely with a cocktail in hand. Alice was just the same. This story didn't feel right.

"Something has happened," she said to Mat. "What are we going to do?"

Her experience as mayor of Salisbury kicked in. She knew people in high places and she wasn't afraid to approach them. Within minutes of learning her sister was gone, Barrie was on the phone with Wicomico County Sheriff Mike Lewis.

Then, Barrie called Ellen. She had to.

"What do you mean?" At first, Ellen didn't understand, but as Barrie explained the details she had, the picture began to take shape. Perhaps Alice just went to see their cousin, Leslie Hickok? But no, Alice wasn't with Leslie or anyone on that side of the family.

Ellen had watched enough television and had seen plenty of movies to know the spouse is always a suspect, but Ellen's mind did not immediately go there. Instead, she wondered if Alice had had it with Jess. Maybe Alice got a hotel room for a few days. But then there was her car. And her cats. She left those behind too, which didn't feel right. The longer Ellen sat with her thoughts, the greater the possibility of his involvement became and the more she realized that she wouldn't put anything past Jess Davis.

• • • • •

Building a Timeline

The police continued investigating through Monday and into Tuesday. The detectives from the Wicomico Bureau of Investigation began an exhaustive search for clues to Alice's whereabouts. They found several surveillance cameras in strategic locations. They looked up the cell phone records for her and Jess. They interviewed family, friends, and neighbors. They even established a tip line. Every effort went into building a timeline of Sunday's events, and it went like this:

Jess and Alice had had visitors that afternoon, Holly Clauss and Lee Love, a former Maryland State Trooper. While they were there, Jess received a phone call at 2:52 p.m. and told the unknown caller he would call them back. One minute later, someone called Alice's cell phone but it went to voicemail. Holly and Lee left the residence around 3:00 p.m.

This is the last time anyone other than Jess saw Alice Davis alive.

One detective discovered security cameras on the exterior of How Sweet It Is, a roadside produce market in Eden, Maryland, about four miles from the Davis home. At 4:35 p.m., one camera recorded a car that looked like Alice's royal blue Honda Fit heading southbound on Route 13. Half an hour later, that same vehicle approached How Sweet It Is and was caught on camera again.

At 5:27 p.m., Jess used Alice's cell phone and dialed into her voicemail. The call was recorded on the West Post Office Road cell phone tower.

Seventeen minutes later, from his own cell phone, Jess called his sister, Patricia Slocum. At 6:00 p.m., Jess called Bailey's Taxi Service, a local cab company.

Nine minutes later, another security camera — this time from the Big Lots store — recorded the blue Honda Fit heading through the parking lot toward the Hunan Chinese restaurant. (People dining at the restaurant later said they remembered police officers asking if any of them had seen Alice Davis.)

At 6:21 p.m., Jess called Bailey's again and five minutes later, a security camera recorded a white minivan (the taxi) pulling up to the Big Lots store. When the taxi driver was later interviewed, he told police he had picked up a middle-aged white man who said he'd just been at a bar, which made sense to him because the guy smelled of alcohol. The driver informed his new passenger that he had to pick up an additional fare at Walmart. At 6:33 p.m., across the highway, Walmart security cameras captured the white minivan with a white male fitting Jess's description in the passenger seat. The other fare never showed up so the taxi driver headed toward Allen. His passenger was chatty, talking about his young Latina girlfriend. When they reached Allen, the passenger asked to be dropped off in front of the post office. As the taxi driver drove away, he glanced up in his rear view mirror and saw the man cross the street.

Cell phone records show that Jess called his voicemail and then his sister again at 6:45 p.m. He made these two calls on his own cell phone, but then he used Alice's cell phone to call Mary Starnes twice, just before 7:00 p.m. And then finally the 911 call occurred at 7:21 p.m., originating from the Davis residence.

Cell phone records, surveillance footage, and witness interviews bolstered the timeline and every piece of evidence indicated Jess Davis was lying to police. Alice's purse, wallet, and cell phone were in the house. The police found Jess's wallet in the driver's side door panel as well as fresh grass in the Honda's undercarriage and brown clumps of hair in the trunk. The lynchpin came when they reviewed the footage from Walmart. Jess had told Deputy Taylor he last saw Alice at 6:30 p.m., but they knew this was a lie because they had him on video at Walmart sitting in the passenger seat of a Bailey's taxi at precisely that same time. They had him.

● ● ● ● ●

The Essential Task

On Tuesday morning, at 7:15 a.m., Micah Stauffer, the principal of Parkside High School, stood in front of the faculty. He had a grim task ahead of him. The day before, Micah had been running errands with his family when he received a phone call from Captain Babe Wilson of the Wicomico County Sheriff's Office. He wanted to know if Micah knew Alice Davis. Micah told him she was one of his English teachers. Then Captain Wilson asked him a startling question, "Is she the type of person who would just leave and not tell anyone her whereabouts?"

"No, actually, she is just the opposite. She's very structured and routine. She's the last person to do something like that."

The remainder of the call was grim. Alice's husband had reported her a missing person. She left for a store and never returned, but her car had been found. Micah was stunned. *Alice Davis is missing?!* It was so out of the realm of normal as to be beyond belief. He felt like he had suddenly found himself at the beginning of *Dateline* episode. That kind of thing happens to other people out there in the world. Not to people you know. Certainly not people like Alice Davis.

Micah, a man of structure and routine himself, knew he had two immediate responsibilities: he arranged for a substitute teacher for her class and he called for a faculty meeting first thing in the morning before the students were set to arrive at school. As principal, he knew it was his duty to provide leadership for the staff and students because this was an unprecedented moment.

Micah Stauffer first met Alice Davis when he came to Parkside as a science teacher in 1998, but he didn't really get to know her until he came back in 2009 as the principal where his first impression of Alice was that she was a bit unapproachable. Perhaps it was her reputation for her high expectations and strong work ethic. Micah felt a formal distance, a kind of reserved manner about her. She wasn't the kind teacher to talk about anything other than the job and Micah didn't push. But his first impression of Alice as a tough taskmaster changed very early on their relationship when he asked for her help on a project. Immediately, he saw her soften, and Alice responded, "Oh! Absolutely!" She was extremely willing to help, to do whatever was necessary to help the students. From that day forward, he saw her in a different light. Where once he thought he saw a coolness, he now had full view of her steadfast dedication to being a teacher and department head. Alice was always ready to do her part — for the students, for her fellow teachers, for the curriculm, and for Parkside. And, as his speech reviewer, Alice never failed to take a red pen to his work. He thought she secretly enjoyed doing that. They had developed a relationship of mutual respect, and certainly admiration on his side.

And there he now stood, on a somber Tuesday morning, looking into the horrified eyes of her co-workers and confirming the terrible news many of them had only just heard. Alice Davis was missing and no one had any idea where she might be. Micah's words landed especially hard for the English department. Alice was their department chair, their stalwart leader, a veteran who once tossed a Board of Education supervisor out of her classroom because the timing of his presence didn't suit her. Micah told them all he knew and tried to inspire hope and faith in them, but he could tell they were just as blindsided and upset by the news as he was.

One of those English teachers sitting in that faculty meeting was Aimee Yeingst. She had already heard about Alice's disappearance from her best friend, Christel Savage, who was also the vice principal at Parkside. Christel told Aimee that Jess Davis was the one who had reported Alice as missing. The moment Aimee hung up the phone, she had only one thought: *Jess Davis.*

He was still on her mind as she sat in the faculty meeting, surrounded by her peers. Everyone remained in absolute silence as they listened to Micah. Aimee sat there, filled with dread and panic, and kept wondering, *what did he do?* She knew Alice and this wasn't like her at all. She was too regimented — she'd never abandon her job, her students, or her teachers. But Aimee knew Jess, and that was a different story.

In the late 1990s, Aimee Yeingst walked into Parkside High School as a student teacher assigned to Alice Davis's classroom. As a soon-to-be graduate of Salisbury University, Aimee needed this opportunity in Alice's class to be successful because her first attempt at student teaching at the middle school level had not gone very well. Being around new people often made Aimee uncomfortable, and likely as a result, Aimee was nervous and unsure of herself in the classroom. Teaching English wasn't even her first or second career choice. But once she met Alice, her fears and worries dissipated. Alice supported her and did anything and everything she could to help Aimee learn how to negoitate a classroom, find structure in lesson planning, and gain confidence in herself as a teacher. Aimee had a true mentor in Alice, a champion who eventually argued, directly to the members at the Board of Education, for Aimee Yeingst to be hired at Parkside at the start of the school year immediately following her successful stint of student teaching.

Once a full-fledged member of the faculty, Aimee soon met Alice's husband at various events and school functions. He seemed nice enough at first, but that quickly changed. Whenever Alice was out of earshot, he would make innuendoes and sexual comments to her and try to touch her. One time he commented on the size of her breasts; another time, he called her on the phone just to chat. His behavior bothered her, both because it was creepy and because Aimee loved and respected Alice, a woman who had become like a second mother to her after the sudden and tragic deaths of her parents. Out of her deep admiration for Alice and growing dislike of Jess, Aimee purposefully avoided having contact with him.

As Micah Stauffer brought the faculty meeting to a close and promised to keep them informed of any new developments, Aimee tried to collected herself and her thoughts. *Where was Alice? What had happened to her?* It was like living inside a nightmare. As Aimee walked down the halls of Parkside, a strange, unsettling reality began to set in. Someone else would be standing in Alice's room. She thought about how Alice ate lunch every day with Susan Westover-Huff. With each step, everything felt wrong and strange, as though the world had been flipped upside-down … Alice was gone and Aimee was sure Jess Davis had something to do with it.

But she couldn't focus on that, not entirely. There was an essential task at hand — teaching. The very task to which Alice had dedicated her entire life. The very task Alice had inspired and encouraged Aimee to pursue. *The most essential task.* Soon, the students would be arriving. They would have questions. Aimee would have a few answers, but not to the most important questions: *Where is Mrs. Davis? What's going on? What happened to her?* Aimee braced herself.

As the students began filing in, Micah Stauffer addressed Alice's class. They had only been with her a week for an hour a day. Just five hours. But it had been enough for her students to recognize they had a really good teacher. After Micah left, several of Alice's students sought out Aimee. They were concerned and scared. They didn't understand. One student burst into tears, and Aimee offered consolation and comfort, a steady hand and reassurance, just as Alice — the teacher and the mentor — had done so many times before.

That was a hard day for Aimee Yeingst. That day broke her heart.

•　•　•　•　•

Wildfire

Tuesday morning saw the story of Alice's disappearance ignite across social media and news outlets, making headlines all over the Delmarva Peninsula. She was the lead story on WBOC and WMDT television stations. "Missing Woman's Car Found" was the headline for the *The Daily Times*, Salisbury's daily newspaper. The bold words set our community on edge, a community unaware of the details police were rapidly uncovering. All we knew was that she was missing and our collective panic was real. Accounts of her disappearance ran like a wildfire through dry brush as people began sharing the news stories and making personal posts, and each one of those set off another spark.

We were all finding out in different ways. Gale Glasgow Dashiell, Alice's childhood best friend, found out when her husband, Dean, handed her the morning paper. Her heart froze in her chest when she saw Alice's picture on the front page. "Oh Alice," she said as she wept. Other people found out when they saw her on a Facebook post or on the morning television programs. And then there were people who, just like me, had concerned family members call to break the news.

Kelly Hager was at her job when she got an urgent call from her mother. Kelly was a web producer for WJZ-TV in Baltimore, Maryland. When she got on the line, her mom told her Alice Davis, Kelly's former English teacher, was missing. The words didn't seem real. *Not Mrs. Davis.* That made no sense.

Immediately, Kelly began scouring the internet for details. Her job as a web producer was to obtain and arrange the news content for the station's website and here she was, posting about the disappearance of her high school English teacher. Everything about it was surreal. She went to the station managers and tried to get them to send a reporter down to cover the story, but there was little interest. Kelly reached out to her contacts at WMDT in Salisbury, the ABC news affiliate where she had worked after graduating from Salisbury University. Her friend was the news manager there and provided her updates and early information. But it wasn't enough. She continued to Google Alice's name and scroll through Facebook.

Kelly thought of Mrs. Davis. All she could remember were the good parts: Alice's kindness, her dry and clever wit, the way she staunchly supported Kelly's love of books. She was a teacher who challenged her — college prep courses were cakewalks compared to Mrs. Davis's English class. Alice connected with Kelly in a way few teachers had, and it made her unforgettable.

In one of her digging sessions, she came across a *Huffington Post* article about Alice and made the inevitable mistake of reading the comments. Anonymous and far-flung internet trolls posted terrible things about Alice, even critiquing the outfit she was last seen wearing. Complete strangers conjured up theories about Alice's culpability in her own murder: *Why didn't she just leave? She must have known better. Had she provoked him in some way?* This infuriated Kelly … as if women need to apologize for what happens to them at the hands of terrible men. These people didn't even know her. They didn't care about Alice the way her community did, the way her students did. Their flippant cruelty broke Kelly. She sat at her computer, feeling waves of anger and despair and sadness wash over her, and she wept.

The commentary pendulum was all over the place: *Had she simply walked away from her life? How could a woman like her just vanish? Was she kidnapped? Or worse? Was there a killer roaming Wicomico County?* Indeed there was. And the police and the detectives knew just who it was.

•   •   •   •   •

A Trail of Deception

Formed in 2001, the Wicomico Bureau of Investigation was a combined investigative unit, comprising agents from the Wicomico County Sheriff's Office and Maryland State Police. The focus of this mutual aid arrangement was major crimes like sexual assaults and homicides. Although Alice's case initially came into the Sheriff's Office as a missing persons report, the elements surrounding it were suspicious enough to warrant the WBI homicide team's involvement. Part of that homicide team were two determined women from the Maryland State Police: Corporal Sabrina Metzger and Detective Sergeant Chastity Blades.

Metzger, who had been with MSP for 12 years, remembered Jess from the 2009 burglary report. It had been almost two years since her last encounter with him. Although she was never able to close that case, she remained convinced he was the one behind it. Suspicion was one thing, hard evidence another. Metzger recalled Alice too. She remembered going to Parkside to interview her and wondering why a lady like Alice was married to a schemer like him. Now, here she was investigating Alice's disappearance and every strange feeling she had about Jess returned in full measure.

Unlike Metzger, Blades had no prior history with Jess Davis, but it was just as clear to her that Jess was their man. Blades was a seasoned cop with 17 years with the Maryland State Police, five of which in homicide. Sheriff Lewis once praised her tenacity and proficiency by saying, "She's a bulldog and damn good."

The search for Alice Davis and the truth of what happened to her rested on the shoulders of two determined women who weren't the least bit scared of Jess Davis.

During the afternoon of Tuesday, September 6th, 2011, Jess had his initial interview at the Wicomico County Sheriff's Office. They read him his Miranda rights and he signed his name to the accompanying paperwork. When the detectives pressed him, he defaulted to a victimized position: "I can't believe you'd think I have something to do with his." But by that time, they had the video surveillance and the premonitory discoveries in Alice's car so they knew he was lying to them. Metzger and Blades confronted him with the mounting evidence. Yet Jess Davis was unmoved. He offered non-answers and tossed out meaningless red herrings. They countered each and every lie with indisputable facts and proof. The game was on and their subject showed no signs of folding.

Metzger and Blades thought it was time for a different approach.

Wicomico County Sheriff Mike Lewis had some optimism going into the interview room. He had known Jess Davis for three decades and he hoped he could use that connection to get Jess to talk to him. Before he entered the interrogation room, he took off his gun, extra magazines, and spare handcuffs. It's a maneuver used by law enforcement to make witnesses feel more at ease and less intimidated. But Jess wasn't an average suspect for Lewis. This man had been a family acquaintance and Lewis hoped he could leverage their relationship, especially when Jess appeared happy to see him. The two men embraced, and Lewis opened the conversation, "I'm so sorry about Alice."

Then the interview took a turn. Lewis began to lay out once more all the details of their case against him. Jess became uncomfortable. The game was changing. Maybe this was a moment in which Jess realized his error in dismissing Metzger and Blades. This was now one alpha male sizing up another alpha male. In Lewis, Jess had a rival who understood the patience and skill required to ensnare his prey. The tension was high. The sheriff was prodding, but the suspect wasn't relenting. Jess repeated his claims: he didn't know what had happened, he loved her, he wouldn't do anything to harm her. Lewis narrowed his steely gaze on Jess, pinning him under the weight of his presumed guilt, and said, "If you didn't kill her, then you were with the person who did."

A tiny fissure started to develop. Jess said he was thirsty and asked for a bottle of water. Lewis obliged, thinking maybe he was starting to crack. He watched as Jess gulped down the water and then paused. The pause felt important. Jess reached for the water again and took another drink. Another pause. Lewis thought, *he's gonna break. I've got him where I want him.*

But then: "Mike, I don't know what happened. I don't know where she is." That was all he was going to give. Jess stopped talking.

The collapse of the interview was frustrating and disheartening for the sheriff. It was clear to him Jess was lying. There was no emotion, no tears, nothing to reveal a man who was devastated over his wife's disappearance. There was only a trail of deception.

As Sheriff Lewis stood to leave the interrogation room, he looked back at Jess and said, "There are no other suspects in this investigation. We know you killed her."

Any relief Jess may have felt with his performance with Lewis was about to be short-lived because, while he may have thought he was one step ahead of everyone else, there was one move for which he hadn't yet prepared: Judge W. Newton Jackson had signed a search warrant for their house and Jess wasn't going home. For the moment, he was knocked out of the game and bounced into a cheap motel.

Built in the 1940s, the Temple Hill Motel was once a pristine mom-and-pop roadside lodge, the kind you might see on Route 66 with alluring neon and freshly painted, bright red doors. The tall signage offered vacancies as well as a pool, AC, and HBO. Located on Route 13, the motel sat on the stretch of highway where the town of Salisbury seamlessly blended into the town of Fruitland, a spot where nearby streets had charming names like Kay, Honeysuckle, Dogwood, and Pine Bluff and were overshadowed by round topped trees. But the Temple Hill Motel's better years had passed and it was now a seedy roadside stop for transients, migrant workers, and prostitutes. Like everything else around Jess Davis, the Temple Hill Motel was something that had once been beautiful and full of possibility but now was irrecoverably damaged and doomed to decomposition.

He waited there until daybreak.

•   •   •   •   •

Over the Tip Line

The tip line sizzled with information. Callers reported sightings of buzzards in the fields near Harcum Wharf Road and around a large marshy area by Cooper Road. Did the police know about the turkey vultures near the telephone poles on Allen Road or behind the Kmart in Salisbury or next to the large dirt pile behind

Denny's? Several people called to offer suggestions of where to look. Had they checked his property on Collins Wharf Road or his hunting spot off Clyde Ford Road across from the waste station in Westover? Even Jess's sister, Patricia Slocum, offered up a possible location: when she would come to visit, Jess would take her to Cokesbury — between Pocomoke and Princess Anne — and she remembered the woods were thick back there.

A man called to suggest that Jess, being a taxidermist, had done the same to her and then put her in the septic system. Even a psychic called, but the dispatcher made no notes of that particular report, other than "psychic called." The only tip that was remotely close to accurate was a man who said he had a dream about Alice and that she was in a dump.

Another caller worked at a doctor's office and suggested the police investigate Jess's medical history, a possible nod to Jess's use of prescription pain pills. An unnamed man reported Jess as a poacher. One caller said he occasionally drank beer with Jess and that he'd been acting strange for the past few weeks. A previous co-worker from his days at Salisbury University said that he was a womanizer and a braggart and may have even contracted AIDS.

There was one caller who offered an interesting glimpse into Jess Davis. A prominent local lawyer who had once been Wicomico County's District Attorney named Davis Ruark called to say that Jess had stalked one of his female clients just a few months prior. How the woman and Jess met was unclear. Ruark said Jess propositioned her for sex, but she refused; then Jess found her on Facebook and also began calling her repeatedly, which forced the woman to change her phone number. Ruark said his client was willing to come forward if necessary.

There were also reported sightings of Alice coming through the tip line. She was walking in the tall grass on Dagsboro Road and turned left down Rum Ridge Road just north of Salisbury. A black man and Alice were in a Chrysler 300 at the Fruitland Walmart two days after she'd been reported missing. A woman called to say she saw Alice looking at cosmetics in a store.

But at the very bottom of one of the tip sheets was a report from a caller who said they were friendly with Jess and had spoken with him since Alice had gone missing. What Jess said to the caller was ominous: "I hope they don't go to Somerset County."

• • • • •

"I don't coddle murderers."

On Wednesday, September 7th, 2011, the police executed a search warrant at about 11 a.m. and went through the entire Davis house searching for evidence. They found and took some of his clothes, an Acer laptop, three cell phones, a GPS unit, his passport, her Last Will and Testament and Power of Attorney paperwork, live ammunition, an Oral-B toothbrush, two hairbrushes, and discarded hair in a bathroom trash can likely pulled from a hairbrush. While they searched the house, they also noted the couple's financial statements, several prescription receipts from a local pharmacy, and Alice's clip-on teacher ID badge for Parkside High School. In total, twenty items were seized from the house and processed into evidence along with what they had already found in her car.

Meanwhile, the officers assigned to surveil him at the Temple Hill Motel saw Jess peeking out of the curtains of Room 131. One said it appeared as though he was scanning the parking lot. He finally emerged from his room, carrying a black bag full of his medications, and headed out on foot toward Kay Avenue. The officers followed him as he then headed south on Camden Avenue. To the surveillance team, it seemed like he was walking home — something they could not allow him to do. Metzger and another detective intercepted Jess and struck up a conversation.

While standing in the street, Jess pulled his insulin pen from the black bag and gave himself a dose. Another Maryland State Trooper, Mark White, pulled up. He also knew Jess Davis. As they all stood talking in the road, Jess told them he wanted to kill himself. That was a major warning sign. Metzger told Jess she was going to take him to Peninsula Regional Medical Center, which is standard protocol any time law enforcement officials come into contact with a person who says or indicates they want to harm themselves. White reinforced Metzger's position and told Jess, "You're going to the hospital either by car or by ambulance." And with that, Jess got into White's car.

One can only speculate what happened during his nearly five-hour hospital stay. Patient records are protected under federal law. Metzger, and later Blades, weren't party to any conversations between Jess and the doctor and hospital staff. He was released into his own custody and, at around 3:00 p.m., he was discharged from the hospital, no longer considered a threat to himself or others.

Metzger and Blades offered Jess a ride home and he accepted. They tried to make small talk with him along the way. Metzger's hope: *Maybe he's going to break. Maybe he's getting tired of this.*

Jess opened up a little and spoke about their cats. Not a word about Alice.

Blades wasn't having it. "Well, if you love your cats, then you might want to find someone to take care of them because you're going to jail for murder."

Jess said nothing.

"You are going to jail for killing your wife."

Jess snapped back at her, "And you ought to be nicer to me!" He said she was being mean and mentally abusive.

"See, this is what's wrong with society. You're a murderer and I don't coddle murderers."

The drive continued. Blades decided to switch her tactic and appeal to his narcissism. "Look, you do taxidermy. You know what heat does to exposed remains. Let her family have her, bury her."

He didn't flinch. He remained as stony as ever.

As Metzger pulled up in the driveway, Blades tried one last time as he got out of the car: "Even if you don't want to admit it, then just call in anonymously and tell us where she is. Just give us closure."

Jess shut the car door and walked inside the house.

●　　●　　●　　●　　●

"We are watching you."

Within hours, Sheriff Lewis held a press conference and announced the investigation had turned from a missing persons report into criminal investigation. He gave a few details about the "rapidly evolving" investigation, but he would not elaborate. He said the car had been found and searched, but did not reveal the findings. Bloodhounds and cadaver dogs were searching the wooded areas of northern Somerset and southern Wicomico counties. The Maryland Department of Natural Resources was assisting the search. There was even a helicopter patrolling the skies above. Every effort was being made to find Alice Davis. He implored local residents, especially those with horses and ATVs, to search their own properties for any signs of Alice, and as always, anyone with information should come forward immediately.

The sheriff stopped just short of what everyone was thinking: they had a suspect.

The message was clear, and if Jess Davis was watching, the

message was pointed at him. Sheriff Lewis wanted it that way. Although he considered it a long shot, Lewis hoped that maybe if Jess knew the community was aware of the suspicions and if he could no longer hide behind his lies and denials, then perhaps he'd come clean. *What would it take*, Lewis wondered? All he could do was wait and watch and keep the pressure on their one and only suspect, which was the very reason there was a deputy stationed across the street from the Davis residence. As Sheriff Lewis would later say, "We didn't try to be covert about it. We wanted him to know: *We are watching you.*"

• • • • •

"Out, out damned spot!"

Jess Davis was running out of time. He paced, back and forth, around the kitchen and through the living room. The humidity of the summer air amplified the tension in the house as well as the acrid smell of the unchanged litter boxes for their five cats. The air was thick in his throat, as if his choices were trying to suffocate him. His head buzzed with the electricity of panic. It filled his body, revealing itself in his wild, protuberant blue eyes. There was nowhere to go, no place to hide, nothing to do but wait for the inevitable. The police would soon be at his door. With each passing second, he knew what was coming: a pair of handcuffs, an accusation of murder, and a life in prison. No more Yangeri or trips to the Dominican Republic. All those plans were lost now. Jess was losing control and the weight of his world was crushing him.

Baser instincts took over. Ensnared animals have been documented chewing off their own feet or legs or tails to escape traps. Jess was no different now, no different than a wounded animal with its leg caught in a set of metal jaws. His predicament, equal parts confining and frantic, afforded him only one viable solution.

Jess found a blue pen and sticky note with a cartoon cat on it. In lopsided and irregular print, he scrawled: "To Whom It May Concern MD State Police did this to my house." And then on the back side: "Tore up everything." He stuck the note to a kitchen cabinet.

Wearing nothing but his underwear, a pair of pale blue cotton boxer shorts, he walked into the living room. He picked up a pack of disposable Schick Extreme3 disposable razors and thought about his next steps. Instead of choosing a knife from their kitchen, Jess disassembled one of the razors in the package and took two of its blades. With one of the blades held between his fingers, he pushed it deep into his left arm, near his elbow, and pulled it across his skin in a short motion. Twice. The blood came quickly.

With the blood dripping down his arm, he headed for the back door, leaving a trail of red, nickel and dime-sized dots on the hardwood living room floor. He made sure the back door was unlocked before returning to the living room. As he walked through the kitchen, where he posted his bizarre accusation on a Post-It Note and where Alice's white tea kettle still sat on the stove, he stepped barefoot in his own blood and smeared it across the white linoleum floor. The droplets, now quarter-sized, were evident near the refrigerator and on the black and white kitchen rug, which was in the shape of a cat's face, whiskers and all.

On a shelf, he saw a little red and black handheld camcorder. Still bleeding, he grabbed it and pushed record as he walked around their living room. The video camera swung wildly as he paced, moving about the room in such a way that his blood covered nearly every surface. Like a macabre game of connect-the-dots, it speckled the wood floor so cared for by Mary Belle. It hit the walls and slid down like tear drops. The house, once the backdrop for so many happy Parsons memories, was becoming a scene from a horror movie.

Jess sat down in his recliner and propped up his feet as casually as he might have done to watch evening television or a football game. A moment passed and he turned off the camcorder. He picked up his cell phone and dialed his sister. The call went to voicemail. He left her a message, telling her that he loved her. "I don't think I'll be here much longer," he said. "I don't have much time and I just wanted to say goodbye."

The blood trickled from his punctured arm, ran down the side of the brown leather chair, and began to pool on the floor next to him. He laid the razor on a decorative end table … the very one that held TV remotes and half-read books and Alice's school papers and, long ago, Casey or Mary Belle's evening cocktail. His blood continued to spill, oozing into the Oriental rug … the very same one seen in Parsons family photographs underneath once-loved pets and toothy, crawling babies.

In his madness, Jess grabbed a blanket and placed it over his wounds.

And then he waited.

•   •   •   •   •

Shortly after 8:00 p.m., Matthew Collier and Ashley Chase, who was also a hunting buddy and friendly with Jess, pulled into the narrow driveway of 3574 Allen Road. But before they had time to shut off their trucks, the deputy was behind them and demanded to know who they were and why they were there.

"I'm just a friend and he called me and we came up to see him," he explained.

"What are you going to do?" asked the deputy.

Matthew hadn't come all that way just to hang out in the drive-way. "I'm going inside."

The deputy allowed it, but the tension was apparent.

Matthew Collier had been in Myrtle Beach, South Carolina on vacation with his family. Early in the week, he listened to his voice-mail and heard a strange message from his old friend, Jess Davis. It was about Alice. Jess said she had left the house but never came back and the tone of Jess's voice had an odd tenor to it. Something didn't add up. He knew Alice wouldn't just disappear like that, vanish into thin air without a word or a whisper.

When Matthew finally spoke to Jess, he sounded terribly upset as he reiterated the same nonsensical story of Alice's disappearance. Matthew listened but Jess's voice didn't ring true to him. They had been friends since the old days at Don's Bella Donna and Matthew knew when Jess was bullshitting him. Matthew ended the call by saying he'd continue to check on him.

But the situation nagged at him and so Matthew decided to leave South Carolina and head for Maryland. He cared deeply for both Jess and Alice, and there was obviously a problem. He felt compelled to go. On his way there, he reached out to Ashley Chase and they agreed to meet at Jess's house in Allen.

Matthew did not know what was going on but he knew enough to know Jess wasn't being straight with him and Matthew's concern for Alice only grew. Jess had once been the kind of man who would lend a hand to anybody, a man who would crack a dumb joke just to make you smile and feel better if you were having a bad day ... the kind of man who, upon finding an orphaned, orange and white kitten in the woods, gingerly scooped it up, held it to his chest, and took it home to his wife. So whatever was going on with Jess and Alice, it felt like serious trouble. The deputy in the driveway only reinforced that feeling.

Matthew and Ashley walked around back and checked the back door. It was unlocked. They opened the door and called out for Jess. No answer. Matthew looked down and saw drops of blood.

Oh no, he thought.

Matthew peeked around the corner into the living room and saw Jess, lying motionless in the recliner. They called his name several times, but again, there was no answer.

Oh no.

Matthew and Ashley ran back to the deputy. Within minutes, the house was sectioned off in crime scene tape. Law enforcement officers were coming in from all over the county as the news of Jess Davis's apparent death was spreading quickly. Matthew and Ashley were detained for statements; their photographs would later appear in the case file along with pictures of the bloody house and Jess's body. Matthew and Ashley were eventually released, along with the news that the prime suspect in Alice's case was dead.

A gruesome scene greeted police and detectives as they began arriving, one after another. Within an hour and a half, there were 17 officials at the house including members of Allen EMS, Detectives Metzger and Blades, Sheriff Mike Lewis, Matthew Maciarello of the Wicomico County State's Attorney's office, and Maryland State Police Lieutenant Ernest Leatherbury, Jr. What they saw was unforgettable and awful.

Jess Davis was nearly naked, covered in his own blood and feces, with his eyes closed and mouth slightly parted on the right side. He lay in the recliner with his bloody feet stretched out before him, knees parted and open like a book. His body, already in the beginning stages of rigor mortis, was cold to the touch and struck a grotesque tableau of jaundice-yellow, cyanosis-blue, and dark red blood.

On the end table next to him was a cell phone, an empty food wrapper, a roll of toilet paper, some spare change, a coaster with a kitten on it, and a bloody razor blade resting on a white doily. In the coagulated blood on the floor next to the recliner was a blanket, a phonebook, and another razor blade. In the air hung a damp stench of cat urine and human waste.

Sheriff Lewis surveyed the scene. It was hard to stomach: even experienced veterans like Leatherbury headed to the back door for air. In the midst of the crime scene, something caught Lewis's eye. A tiny, furtive movement. One of Alice's cats was licking the blood from its paw.

•   •   •   •   •

The next day, Thursday morning, Sheriff Mike Lewis held another press conference. This time, he was flanked by then Wicomico County State's Attorney Matthew Maciarello and Wicomico Bureau of Investigation's Sergeant David Owens. Sheriff Lewis told reporters, "We do believe the man who knows all the facts of the case is deceased at this time. We do believe that. However, we will continue to investigate this case."

The search for Alice continued.

Matthew Collier volunteered to go with the teams looking for her. He thought he could help because he knew many of Jess's hunting spots. Clyde Ford Road. River Road. Charles Cannon Road. He tried to shake the images of the previous night. It was hard to see someone he had known and held as a good friend for three decades, lying in a pool of blood. He needed to do something, anything. And knowing those hunting spots meant that Matthew understood he might just see Alice the same way or worse. But he wanted to find her. He wanted to be the one who helped end the nightmare. At first, the detectives gave him a hard time. One even suggested that maybe Matthew had helped Jess get rid of Alice and now he was there to see what they knew. Matthew took great offense to this. He thought Alice was an angel on earth, a truly good and decent woman; he was there to help. Matthew shot back, half in anger and half in heartache, "Don't do this to me, man." The notion of Matthew's assistance evaporated quickly, though, and the detectives went to all the spots Matthew took them. Alice wasn't in any of them and Matthew began to worry maybe they wouldn't ever find her.

Until a 911 call came in on Sunday afternoon. The caller said there was a body in the woods off Loretto Road.

•   •   •   •   •

The Manner of Death

With his suicide and the discovery of Alice's body, the case appeared to solve itself, culminating in the age-old cliche — the husband did it. But what exactly had he done?

That Sunday afternoon, Jess and Alice entertained two visitors, Holly Clauss and Lee Love. It was the perfect day to be out and about: the temperatures were in the low 80s with a calm and sunny sky. The conversation was friendly and Alice and Jess seemed normal and at ease with each other. There was nothing out of the ordinary, nothing to suggest what would soon unfold. Shortly before 3 p.m., both Alice and Jess's cell phones rang. Jess said he'd call back; Alice never answered, probably because Holly and Lee were getting ready to leave. The couples said their goodbyes and Holly and Lee left the little brick rancher.

Alice was drinking her old standard, a vodka martini. The glass on the table next to her chair was about half-empty. Jess was drinking too. And then the day turned. A darkness came over Jess, but this time he would not pull back.

Maybe they got into an argument. There was no shortage of reasons for them to quarrel. Jess was having an affair with Yangeri, an affair that Jess had said temporarily resulted in a pregnancy and an expectation of a new family. Sometime after the miscarriage, Yangeri had gone back to the Dominican Republic where Jess continued to visit her. Had Alice heard that he was talking about moving there and starting a scooter business? Had she caught wind of the rumor that Jess had purchased a home in the DR, another possible reason for their constant financial hemorrhaging? Alice was committed to selling their home in Allen and moving with him to Canal Woods in Fruitland. They were selling their furniture and vehicles and Jess was asking her friends for loans, but it was never enough. They were broke. They were unhappy together. They wanted different things.

Or maybe not. None of this was news to Alice. She had lived with it for years. His girlfriends, his lies, his hustles: she bore everything, resigned and surrendered to the mess her life had become. Alice was going to stay the course, no matter the cost, and so maybe there was no reason for her to fight with him.

But what is certain is that this otherwise serene summer day erupted into a grotesque maelstrom.

Jess came at Alice with a hammer, swinging hard and wild at her head. She saw it just as it was happening. She raised her left arm, trying desperately to block the attack. He swung again and again, each time the hammer came down, connecting with the left side of her head just behind her ear. After the third blow, Alice's arm dropped.

Her last thoughts must have been full of confusion and despair. Quick and racing. The man she loved with a hammer in his hand.

In this place, her childhood home where she had always been so safe and comfortable. Sharp pain and crushing grief. A heart broken. And then, Alice's world slipped into darkness.

Maybe he had planned it. Maybe he just snapped in a moment of rage, one of those moments in which his ice blue eyes turned as black as ink, only to shrink back when he saw what he had done to Alice, the one woman who always saw the best in him even when he was doing his worst to her.

But he would not call 911. He would not try to save her.

Jess managed to load her lifeless body into the back of the Honda Fit. A clump of her hair caught in the hatchback by the floor panel, an eventual telltale sign to investigators. He drove south along the treelined section of Route 13. Just before he reached Princess Anne, he made a left onto Loretto Road and over the railroad tracks. He passed a church and a granite memorial marker. He made a left onto an unmarked gravel path and headed into the woods, driving parallel to a little stream. Grass and mud caked the underside of the car. Jess kept going, passing miscellaneous bits of trash and litter, until he came to a secluded meadow.

He backed in. Got out. Opened the rear hatch. She was so still. There would be no more laughter, no more dry quips, no more words. Only silence now.

He grabbed her ankles and pulled. Her body slid from the hatchback and landed hard on the ground, face down. Her rib broke. Her sternum cracked. The tip of her left index finger fractured.

He dragged her a short distance away. Her left shoe, a Faded Glory canvas slip-on, fell from her foot. Her shirt bunched up beneath her, exposing her soft belly to the dirt and weeds. And he left her there. Discarded in the trash heaps.

Jess returned to the highway, driving past How Sweet It Is

where he was caught on their surveillance camera at 4:35 p.m. He called his sister. He called his voicemail. He called a taxi. He began to weave several loose threads of a lie into an outright fabrication. His wife was missing, he would say, when the police began to show up at his house.

Sunset came at 7:28 p.m. The greens and blues of twilight gave way to the purple of night as stars lit up the sky above the place where Alice's body began its descent into decay.

Four miles away, Jess was drinking and calling her friends. It was unlike her to be gone for so long, he said. He didn't know where Alice was, he said. He couldn't bear the thought of something bad happening to her, he said. And on and on.

All the dark secrets she kept, the terrible things he had said and done to her over their thirty years together were about to be ushered into the light. Her family and friends, even strangers across the country, would bear witness to her private life, only this time there would be no safeguards, no meticulous bits of armor to keep onlookers at a distance, and there was nothing she could do to stop it. Alice was gone, undone by her fealty to the madman. Her body remained in that little meadow for the next seven days. In the late summer heat and the cool of night. In storms. In morning mist.

Abandoned and alone.

Part IV

"The fault, dear Brutus,
is not in our stars,
but in ourselves ..."

JULIUS CAESAR
ACT I, SCENE ii

Chalk Marks

Sixteen years before the murder of Alice Davis, there had been another notorious murder near Princess Anne. On October 17th, 1995, a young and handsome Maryland State Trooper named Eddie Plank sat in his cruiser and calibrated his radar gun. Earlier that day, he had played racquetball with his friend, a fellow trooper by the name of Mike Lewis. Within hours of that game, Plank would be dead.

His patrol vehicle sat near Perry Road on Route 13 near Princess Anne in Somerset County. The spot was close to his barracks. Nearby, the muddy Manokin River winds like a copperhead snake, dividing the woods between a trailer park and Eastern Correctional Institute, a medium-security prison for men. A narrow concrete bridge allows the river to cross under the highway where the Manokin thins itself into Kings Creek and then trails off only to disappear into patches of farmland, chicken houses, and forested hunting grounds. If you were driving along this stretch of road and happened to blink, you might just miss it all entirely.

With his radar gun ready, he aimed and hit a speeding car driven by Ivan Lovell, who had over half a pound of crack cocaine and a gun in his possession. During the traffic stop, Ivan Lovell did not produce his identification and gave a fictitious name, calling himself Charles Billups. Eddie Plank wrote him two citations: one for speeding and the other for not having a driver's license on him. Then the fatal mistake: Ivan Lovell began to sign his real name instead of Charles Billups, and in the ensuing confusion, Lovell pulled his gun and shot Eddie Plank in the face.

The community mourned the loss of a rising star, a kind and civic-minded hometown boy taken in his prime. Plank was just 28 years old, with a young wife and an infant daughter. Mike Lewis was assigned to a task force to investigate the murder. Plank's family and friends reeled, overwhelmed with shellshock and grief. In the days that followed, the local papers ran various memorial pieces; *The Baltimore Sun* featured a lengthy article in which a reporter spoke to a Somerset County man who was visiting the murder scene. The man's name was Jess Davis. He was standing on the side of the highway, the site of a murder marked by white and yellow flowers and a teddy bear. The reporter noted that the man stared at the scarlet chalk marks left by investigators and that the man said he had only met Plank eight or ten times. "He was always happy, real easy going. He didn't take life's problems as a burden. He liked the bright side of things," said a somber Jess Davis.

It is a strange anecdote, Jess visiting the scene of a murder for a person he held only as the briefest of acquaintances. How could Jess have known what Eddie Plank's approach to life was? Was there something about the murder scene that fascinated Jess? Did curiosity get the better of him? This is pure conjecture, of course, but almost sixteen years later, Jess Davis would kill two people not too far from that very spot. And it would be Plank's friend, Mike Lewis, who would again find himself near the center of another murder investigation involving people he knew. This is often the way it is with small towns and close-knit, rural communities. We are all inexorably intertwined.

Maybe Jess Davis couldn't resist visiting the place where Plank was killed. Did he wonder then, while standing on the highway in that early autumn, what it would be like to take a life? Had the notion of killing, beyond hunting animals, entered his mind before that Sunday in September 2011? In this strange little moment which is barely more than a mention in an old newspaper article, we see a future killer paying some sort of bizarre homage to a murder scene on the side of a busy interstate, riveted by the red outline of a body, a person he barely knew.

This story calls to mind every lingering question left in the wake of Alice's murder at the hands of Jess Davis: what do we make of all this? What happened? How and why? What becomes of the wreckage? And what do we do now?

If you drive that stretch of highway where the Manokin begins to diminish into nothingness, you will come upon a memorial marker honoring two Maryland State Troopers from Princess Anne who lost their lives in the line of duty: Trooper First Class Eric D. Monk, who was hit by a car during a traffic stop, and Trooper First Class Edward A. Plank, Jr. Gone are the white and yellow flowers and the teddy bear. Their names are painted in bold white letters on a brown state highway sign standing in the median and surrounded by generic, commercial landscaping. The highway is dedicated to them, to their service, and to their memory. Untold numbers of cars pass by the signs every day. I wonder how many notice. And of those who do, I wonder how many people are curious to know their stories, curious to know what happened.

This is where I find myself with Alice.

Seven miles north of the highway sign bearing Plank's name is the marker by the church where Alice's body was found, the secluded clearing Jess chose as the place where his wife's body would lay while the rest of us — her family, friends, neighbors, students, teaching community — grieved for her, ached for her, cried and waited for her, haunted by our memories and dumbstruck by the reality of our loss. There will be no markers, no pilgrimages through pokeweeds and mosquitoes to that lonesome, quiet meadow where, instead of an outline on asphalt, there is only the soft passing of time and the colors of the seasons. There is only a sifting through of the stories and memories and a wrenching search for facts amid the fictions.

Now, there is only the chasing of Alice.

• • • • •

A Gathering of Storm Clouds

During those days when Alice was missing, my mind was a mess. I became obsessive, logging into Facebook for updates, pulling up news sites and clicking on anything that bore her name. I could not stop talking about it, about her. It even prompted a fight with my then-husband who was an officer with Salisbury Police Department. I needed to clear my head so I decided to go for a run. I was putting on my running shoes and I was talking about Alice, about how it didn't make sense, about how the whole thing made me sick to my stomach. He sat on the edge of the bed. For a moment, we were both quiet.

And then: "You know they think the husband killed her, right?" It was so casual and clinical. Cops are often this way. They are so accustomed to terrible news and awful people that sometimes they forget the rest of us are not. He had seen dead bodies — decaying, frozen, shot, left in the street, tangled in cars, human lives taken in all manner of ways. But this was new for me and this wasn't just some *body*. This was Mrs. Davis: the woman who wrapped her arms around me when I was a scared young girl. She had been a soft place to fall, and it was a kindness that I would never be able to repay now. If I pinched my eyes together hard enough, I could almost hear her voice, see her at the overhead projector, smiling as she recited Shakespeare …

"Yeah, I do." This was all I could manage through clenched teeth and hot tears. I didn't need facts. I needed understanding and comfort. He was all cop, always on duty. I tied my shoes and hit the door. I ran and ran that day. Nothing helped.

In the middle of the night, I awoke to the sounds of a thunderstorm. I lay in my bed, eyes wide, listening to the winds pick up and the rain drops pelt against the house. A bolt of lightning flashed; a loud thunderous crash followed. I turned over to face the window, to face the coming storm. I have always loved thunderstorms — the anticipation and electric release, the thought of danger lurking on the horizon, the swelling of gray and purple clouds, the low vibrations of distant rolling thunder. Storms have always excited me, comforted me in a way. But this night was different. All I could think of was Alice. *Out there. In the dark, in the rain, in the lightning and thunder. Out there. Presumed dead and absolutely alone.* I remembered her kindness, her smile, all she did for me when I was just a kid in her class. *She doesn't deserve this*, I thought. Beginning in that moment, I knew I would always be haunted by her memory and by what had happened to her.

And then I realized that everyone else who knew her and loved her was going to be haunted too. Memories now tinged bittersweet. Unanswered questions. Words left unsaid. Guilt. Regret. A lifetime of plans and expectations evaporating into the ether.

That same night, miles away on the other side of Salisbury, Barrie Tilghman awoke to the same storm. She saw the lightning and heard the thunder and longed for her little sister left alone in the darkness — a sister now twice lost to her.

•   •   •   •   •

After Alice's body was found, we were left to deal with the fallout, each in our own way. I remained absolutely preoccupied by what had happened to her. I was still compulsively checking social media and local news outlets. An editorial titled "A Community's Tale of Horror" in *The Daily Times* on September 14th, 2011 echoed the sentiments of a community: initial confusion followed by an increasing sense of dread punctuated with fond remembrances and hopes for closure. The editorial praised law enforcement officials for their diligence and thanked them for their hard work. It was a succinct accounting, and soon the news cycle would do what it always does — move on.

But all I wanted was to talk about her. Find information. I needed something, anything, to go on. It was so hard to process her murder and my searches never yielded anything to help me with that. And I wasn't alone. Classmates and teachers were reaching out to one another in real life and on social media; random commenters offered their prayers on news stories about her. We didn't know what to do with our feelings, so much sorrow and anger and guilt. We began pulling out old yearbooks and writing journals, looking for her face and her notes in the margins. When we came together, we hugged one another and we cried. We shared our stories on social media in lengthy posts and wrenching essays. We used our words — the very tool Alice had worked so hard to put in our hands.

Carl Thress, who had known Mrs. Davis as Miss Parsons when he was a freshman enrolled in her creative writing class, dug out his old journal, one he had kept for 27 years. He looked in the margins and found her notes of encouragement. In one entry, he wrote about life being like an escalator with its ups and downs, to which she wrote back: "Mostly I'm on a down escalator trying to get to the top." When he expressed a desire to see his name on the spine of a book of his own, she wrote, "I have a feeling one day you will." Carl's favorite note came at the the end of the journal: "Carl, your writing is always enjoyable to read. Keep at it; you've got what it takes! It has been a pleasure to have you in class." As he sat and re-read those words from Alice Parsons, he felt loss and anger. How could someone do this to her?

In memory of her and her death, Carl wrote a blog post about her, about how writing had always been important to him, but Alice's kind reassurances gave him the boost of self-confidence to begin to see himself as a writer. Alice had helped a young man in love with words, and that young man never forgot her. He lamented that he could not have written a better ending for his teacher who had been so supportive of him. "She deserved far better," he wrote.

• • • • •

On the night of Wednesday, October 5th, 2011, I pulled up to Parkside High School. The parking lot was filling up as scores of people made their way inside for a memorial service for Alice Davis. My heart was a wild bird caught in a cage, thrashing itself against unyielding confines. My stomach was in constant tumult. My mind was running a constant loop of *I shouldn't be here ... we shouldn't be here ... but she should.*

As I walked towards the building, a deluge of old memories nearly buckled my knees. Leah Capcino's orange VW bug parked in the senior lot. Doug Phillips passing me little notes between classes. Volleyball games. Books covered in brown paper bags from the grocery store. Dressing in pleated uniform skirts with my lacrosse teammates for home games. The faces of my teachers. Pizza in the cafeteria. The planetarium.

During the years from 1993 through 1997, when I roamed the hallways in my Birkenstocks and acid washed jeans, it felt like a home away from home. I had friends, I knew my way around, and the teachers were, well, exactly what you'd expect of high school teachers. Upstairs, I had chemistry with Mr. Fred Dinges, whose shock of white hair matched his lab coat. There was Mrs. Rosemary

Heher, a relocated New Yorker who taught geometry in strict and meticulous terms. Mr. James Wilson gave us a laugh everyday as we watched him fold and unfold his greater than six foot frame in and out of a little red Ford Festiva. His class? Physics. Although the upstairs classrooms were primarily for math and sciences, there was one exception. Ms. Anne Collins taught AP US History in the most remote back corner of the second floor. Her stentorian voice and teaching style likely resulted in her classroom location, but Ms. Collins wasn't the kind of teacher to be worried about such things.

Downstairs were the languages and the rest of the social studies classrooms. The first classroom belonged to Mrs. Warwick, who was basically the grandmother of the school. Twenty years later, her students still referred to themselves as "Warwick Kids." Mrs. Cindy Bennett taught civics and AP US Government a few classrooms down. She always reminded me of the kind of lady you'd want to have as a neighbor: organized, friendly, and attentive. Down from her was Mrs. Colleen Dallam, who taught World Civilizations. Every morning, she'd ask us to report on a news item, local or national, and everyday, as a joke, one of us would mention a Perdue chicken truck turning over on the highway. By Christmas, she limited us to non-chicken related news. Mr. Oldham who taught geography was, at that point in my life, the kindest man I'd ever met. The foreign languages — Spanish, French, and Latin — were taught by Mrs. Elizabeth Jones, Mrs. Maria Evans, Mrs. Gladys Goslee, and Mrs. Pat Piper. The only time I ever caught a detention was from Mrs. Elizabeth Jones; my offense was talking without permission and being "repeatedly warned." (She wasn't wrong.) In the English department, along with Mrs. Warwick, there was Ms. Dorothy Yeatman, who endured much of my terrible poetry in her Creative Writing class, Mrs. Dawn Neville, who was a lovely combination of nurturing mother and absent-minded professor, and then there was my favorite — Mrs. Alice Davis, always standing in the hallway, smiling at me.

With each step, I could see where I once was, who I had once been when Alice had been alive and an unforgettable part of my youth. I stood in front of Parkside High School. Gone was the facade of the 1970s. In the years since I'd left, a large vocational wing had been added to the front of the school. Inside the main doors, visitors are now greeted by lofty ceilings and fresh white paint and video cameras — a stark contrast to the taupe colors and acoustic tiles of my Parkside Prison. The renovations were jarring and different. Suddenly my memories were sepia-toned and fading away. My heart ached in that way only nostalgia can render … like the prick of a thorn in the flesh of your palm, drawing just enough blood and sting to make you wince. You pull back and examine how such a small, seemingly insignificant thing can wound you so.

Rooting me to the present were the folded papers in my hand. It was my speech. Days before, Barrie Tilghman had called me. I was surprised to hear from her but equally eager to express my condolences and my sorrow over the loss of Alice. I knew Barrie socially: her husband was the insurance agent for my mother's ambulance company and had been so for a decade or more. When Barrie called, she had a favor — one I would not turn down. Would I speak at the memorial service at Parkside?

As a writer, there are a few times in which you know your words must be perfect. But because you are a writer, you know they won't be. Perfect words rarely come at the right time, if ever at all. You write, you destroy, and you agonize; as the deadline approaches, you do the best you can. You worry yourself sick. You walk away with the best words you can manage at that moment. This was the case with my speech for Alice.

The auditorium was filled to capacity with many more standing in the hallway. Staring at the stage, I had flashbacks of the Junior/ Senior banquets, the annual precursor to the senior prom. Each year, the juniors voted amongst themselves for various superlatives; the "winners" would then buy little gag gifts and award them to a senior of the same category at the banquet. The Barbie and Ken award was for the best couple and Miss Clairol went to the girl who couldn't live without makeup and hair spray. The Bette Davis award was for the prettiest eyes, and of course there were awards for the canonical high school stereotypes: biggest jock, smartest nerd, through-and-through country bumpkin, and funniest class clown. Two years in a row, I "won" the worst driver award; my date, Doug Phillips, got the Casanova award both times. On those nights, the upperclassmen of Parkside High School, all dressed up with fresh corsages and boutonnières, gathered in the auditorium for the "awards" and the jokes and then retired to the cafeteria where we danced under the dimmed fluorescent light bulbs.

But this night, there would be none of those things.

I was in the program between Mrs. Dollie Wright singing *It Is Well With My Soul* and Dr. Carolyn Elmore, a former English supervisor and then member of the Wicomico County Board of Education. When my name was called, I rose and walked to the podium, which was placed in nearly the same spot on the stage as it had been when Alice announced me as the winner of the Old Home Prize. My memories of happier days were smashing up against this current awful reality, and I willed myself to some sort of composure.

I unfolded my speech and began. "Tonight, we have come together to honor our Alice and the beginning of her legacy. We are here because we love her ... and, more importantly, because she loved us." There was a moment when I looked up and out into the crowd. A sea of faces marked by sadness and tears. In the audience sat my best friend, Patty, who came to support me. When I looked at her during my speech, she had tears in her eyes. For a brief second, I remembered it was Patty who told me Alice's body had been found. I was at her house in Fenwick Island when the news broke. She sat me down on the sofa in her sunroom and took my hands in hers. She looked me in the eye and said she was sorry, but she had some bad news for me ....

I focused again and continued, "Perhaps there is no greater purpose than being a teacher: to give so selflessly to others without the expectation of a reward, to impact the lives of young people in such a way that it cannot be forgotten, to share a wealth of knowledge and then to listen as the occasion requires. Truly it is a noble cause and Alice fully embodied the giving spirit of a teacher. She left her indelible mark on all of her students. I am just one of many."

There in that auditorium which had seen thousands of kids come and go — many of them touched by her — the tragedy and absurdity of the entire situation was not lost on us. In that moment, hundreds of people came together and collectively wondered, *just what the hell had happened to Alice Davis?*

Shaking and trying not to cry, I moved through the rest of my speech and then made my way back to my seat. Not a single speaker who took the stage that night could provide any answers. The only two people who could were gone, dead at the hands of Jess Davis. Underneath the despondency of those gathered was an anger ... a frustration we could do nothing with. It was a new burden to bear and it was placed upon us all.

As I walked to my car that night, I turned my back on Parkside High School. It would never again be the playful Parkside Prison it once was to me. Never again would I drive past this place without pangs of sorrow and anger. My memories were tainted now and that would never be undone. Those yearbook moments frozen in grainy black and white photographs cannot be reconciled with the knowledge of what would become of the teacher who saved me.

Barrie Tilghman had one last request for me: to give a eulogy at Alice's funeral. I retooled my memorial speech and arrived at the Emmanuel Wesylan Church in Salisbury on October 8th, 2011. It was a beautiful Saturday — the kind of day in early fall when it still feels warm enough to go to the beach and stick your toes in the sand. The sky overhead was a cloudless blue. It was the kind of perfect day that could inspire children and poets, and even me, had different circumstances existed. Originally her funeral was to be held at the small church in Allen where Alice had grown up and was married, but because the memorial service had such a large attendance, her sisters moved it to a place with a greater capacity.

My revised speech included more memories from her students because this was my job — to speak for her students and her legacy with us. So I sent messages to fellow classmates and friends asking if they would share their memories of Alice.

One of the first people to respond was Ann Lawrence Rives, who recalled her senior-year English class. Ann had procrastinated on her thesis paper and waited until the very last minute to put together a flimsy outline on a superficial topic. Alice saw right through it and knew Ann was better than what she had put forward. The next day, Alice pulled her aside and informed her that the chosen topic was beneath Ann's ability and gave her more time to find a more challenging topic, something that would meet the expectations Alice had. And so Ann did. She got serious about her thesis. Although she had tried to breeze through the assignment, Ann knew her English teacher would not accept lesser-than-expected work. Alice's prodding worked: Ann's thesis won the Old Home Prize that year. In the years after Ann left Alice's classroom, she became a lawyer and a writer.

Barbara Kiviat had been my class's valedictorian, and she remembered, as I did, being a little afraid of Alice because of her
no-nonsense reputation. Barbara sensed Alice sizing her up, esti-
mating her talents, and then pushing her for better work, stronger
writing. At the time, Barbara chalked it up to Alice Davis being a
hard teacher: "It was never about how I stacked up to the other kids
in the class; it was about how I stacked up to what I was capable of.
I don't know how she knew what I was capable of, but she did and
she held me to that. It's only as I've grown older that I've come to
understand that she was tough on us not because she didn't love us,
but because she did." Barbara went on to be a staff writer for *TIME*
Magazine with her own byline and now teaches at Stanford.

And there were others. Tiffany Hoke Vandervoordt pursued a
degree in English because of something she saw in Alice — passion. The spark she had for literature, for words, and for writing
well were inspirational to Tiffany. While being a writer might not
be a job that is always rewarded financially, Tiffany saw in Alice
there was another kind of job satisfaction in loving what you do.
Tiffany told me that she chose to be a writer *because* of Alice. For a
moment, I sat in the church pew, staring at Tiffany's words in my
eulogy speech and I wondered: just how many writers did Alice
nurture in her classroom? How many future authors, journalists,
copy writers, editors, and bloggers would trace their origin stories
back to Alice? There had been countless young faces looking up at
her over the years, students who looked at her and saw a part of
themselves ... a love of words or a passion for books and reading
... and found real comfort in that reflection. I smiled a little bit. It's
like we were a writing army and Alice had been our general.

There was no casket at the funeral. Just a poster of Alice smiling
and some lovely flowers next to the podium. I delivered my eulogy
and tried not to cry. I failed.

Two years after those speeches, I moved away from Salisbury, away from the memories of my childhood and Parkside, away from my old neighborhood and all those things that filled me with these wistful, anguished feelings. I wasn't happy to leave, but I wasn't happy to return either.

It was time to go.

• • • • •

The Blood of the Father

Absent from Alice's memorial service and funeral was Jess's family. Barrie had seen to that. She sent a sharp email to Lori Lopez a week after Alice's body was found, requesting that she not come to the memorial service or the funeral. No one from his side was wanted. Barrie and Ellen were devastated and in pain; they could not bear to look upon the faces of Jess's family. He had murdered their sister. He had taken an aunt from her nieces and nephews and a teacher from her students. He had stolen a woman who was counted as a dear friend to many. They couldn't have such a close link to Jess Davis at her services. There would no be forgiveness, at least not this soon.

The sins of the father had been passed onto the daughter.

The email stung. Lori loved Alice and Alice had returned that love. Their relationship had always been a good one, and it had existed entirely outside the realm of Barrie and Ellen's understanding. At the end, Lori and Alice's relationship had existed outside of Jess, too. Alice had been a kind stepmother to Lori, a thoughtful mother-in-law to Johnny, and loving grandmother to their children. The loss of Alice was just as unimaginable to Lori as it was to Barrie and Ellen, but her grief was multiplied because the murderer was her father.

In the depths of her heartache, Lori acquiesced and kept her distance. She'd have to say her goodbye some other way. So often, there is a shaming mark that falls upon the family of criminals and monsters, and this tainting by familial association is difficult, often impossible to shed, especially in the early days of a tragedy. While Lori understood where Barrie and Ellen were coming from and respected their position, it still hurt. So much of the wreckage seemed to be laid at her feet.

•   •   •   •   •

On the weekend of September 23rd, 2011, Lori and Johnny went to the little brick rancher on Allen Road to begin the process of cleaning up. Lori had inherited everything: insurance policies, the house, the car, everything left inside the house. She found that the house might as well have belonged to a stranger: what had once been the warm and inviting home of a loving set of grandparents now resembled an empty set from a horror film.

The house needed a thorough cleaning. Perhaps even an exorcism. Lori emptied the refrigerator of spoiled food and she aired out the house. The smell of five old cats and a bloody, fecal-stained crime scene had been marinating in the heat and humidity of the late Delmarva summer. (The cats were euthanized, cremated, and buried with Alice who was laid to rest next to Mary Belle and Casey.) The house was emptier than it had been on previous visits, many pieces of furniture were gone, either having been sold or pawned because of the impending house sale.

On the table next to Alice's chair in the living room sat a half-empty martini. Next to the glass was a pair of her earrings. To Lori, it was as if time had stopped, as if Alice simply rose from the chair, and vanished. Lori stared at the glass — the last martini of Alice's life. She also found flight information for an upcoming trip to the Dominican Republic. It looked like Jess was making plans to go again.

But there was an issue of greater urgency: the blood. Her father's blood. It was absolutely everywhere. The phone book on the table next to his chair was filled with coagulated blood. It was embedded into the living room floor. Blood had filled and then dried between the planks of the hardwood floors. Lori and Johnny, on their hands and knees and with each brush stroke, set themselves to one of the hardest tasks imaginable — cleaning up her father's crime scene. In all her life, Lori had never seen so much blood.

Dawn Neville came by to help Lori and Johnny. She went through the house trying to find and save items that Barrie and Ellen and their families might want. Casey's old Navy uniform. Photographs. A watercolor picture of fish in seagrasses painted by Barrie's daughter. It had hung in the kitchen. She set everything aside in a couple of big boxes.

Dawn knew that house. As she looked around, she began to sort through her memories and reconcile them with the knowledge of what happened there. The house wasn't clean. Alice had once been a fanatic about keeping cat hair off every surface. Now, there were huge hairballs under the television and in the corners. The metaphor could not have been more clear: the neglected state of the house paralleled the deterioration of both Alice and her marriage. Despite the outward, normal appearance, something was very wrong on the inside.

In the kitchen, she saw one of Alice's cake stands smashed into pieces. Had that happened in a fight? During the warrant search? Dawn found a bank statement from the end of August on top of the microwave. She studied it. Alice had been paid at the end of the month and there was a withdrawal made the very next day, taking almost every bit of it. Dawn knew what she was seeing. Here was an example of how Jess was bleeding Alice dry financially. He had left her with $36. It hit Dawn in the gut. *Had Alice confronted Jess about it*, she wondered? *Had that started a fatal fight?*

In Alice's bedroom, something else caught her eye — the quilt on Alice's bed. It was facing the wrong direction. Dawn had been with Alice when she purchased the quilt and Alice was specific about how it was to lay on the bed. As she stood in Alice's bedroom, she felt uneasy because she knew Alice would not have made her bed that way. Her unease doubled when Lori told Dawn that she had seen a bunch of Kleenex with mascara marks on them in the wastebasket in Alice's bedroom. Had Alice been crying? Did any of this mean something in a larger context? Or were these things — the cake stand, the bank statement, the quilt, the mascara-stained Kleenex — all irrelevant? Were they unrelated to the immediate crime but rather just symptoms of a marriage spiraling out of control?

Dawn struggled to understand, to make sense of the senseless. There were so many memories running through her mind and she tried to piece them together, hoping she might unlock the mystery of what had happened to Alice. And there was one moment that now haunted Dawn.

Just before her trip to Big Bend, Oregon that Labor Day Weekend in 2011, Dawn had reached out to Alice and asked her if she wanted to go see a movie. *The Help* was playing at the theater in Salisbury. Dawn knew Alice would like it and much to Dawn's happy surprise, Alice said she'd go. This was very unusual: Alice had been withdrawing more from her friends and turning down invitations, a pattern dating back to when Casey died. But this movie night was a rare moment and Dawn seized it. They met at the theater and Dawn bought their tickets.

After the movie was over, the two women walked to their cars:

Dawn's Toyota Prius was right next to Alice's Honda Fit. Alice thanked Dawn for inviting her to the movie and pulled $7.50 from her pocket to pay Dawn for her ticket.

"Oh, keep your money," Dawn said.

Alice refused. "Take it and when you get back from Oregon, we'll go out and have a drink and then you can treat." Dawn could hardly believe her ears. *This is more like the old Alice!*

Dawn looked in the back seat of Alice's car and saw the seats were folded down. She remarked to Alice about it.

"Jess insists on having them down," Alice said as she opened the door and pushed the seats back up.

More than the knowledge of the details of the murder, more than seeing downturned seats as a symbol of Alice's fate, Dawn now had a clear view of just how wrong things had gone and how far out of control Alice's life had become. She remembered the beginning of her friendship with Alice and how youthful she had been. Dawn recalled that the first time she met Jess Davis was at the house of a fellow teacher, Sandy Greer, who was the department head at Parkside. Sandy would invite the entire English department over to her house and everyone brought a little something — appetizers, drinks, a dessert. The parties were for unwinding and having a little fun. This was in the early 1980s; Alice, a new teacher at Parkside, got an invite to Sandy's party. On Alice's arm was Jess Davis and she introduced him to the group as her boyfriend. Dawn never forgot that because it seemed so innocent for an almost 30-something Alice to introduce her beau to the group in that way. It was the quaintness of the word "boyfriend." At that age, other teachers were "shacking up" but not Alice Parsons. There was something naive and wholesome about her and this boyfriend. Even Mary Starnes remarked about it to Dawn, saying "Wasn't that sweet?" Jess made a good impression at the party; he cracked a few jokes and seemed at ease. They appeared happy together — Alice, rosy-cheeked with a charming smile and lovely blue eyes … Jess, boisterous and convivial with his working man's hands and blue collar swagger. Everyone at the party thought they were a nice young couple, just getting their start in the world.

But then Dawn's mind would fast-forward to the murder and a dozen other memories would flood in. Like the moment when Alice was still missing and Dawn was driving down Route 13. Feeling desperate, she silently asked Alice for a sign. *Where are you?* Just then, a couple of buzzards flew across the road in front of her. *They come for death*, she thought. Was this a sign or merely a natural occurrence? Whether it was confirmation or coincidence, the sight broke her heart. Dawn wept as she drove.

Looking back, Dawn could see how Jess and Alice's relationship was moving in an ill-fated arc. Alcohol and drugs. Extra martial affairs and financial bleed outs. Her seclusion and his capriciousness. To think of how much their lives would change from that first introduction at Sandy Greer's party to buzzards on a highway … this was such a tragedy.

• • • • •

Monsters and Hurricanes

As 2011 was drawing to a close in late December, *The Daily Times* ran a Top 10 list of their major stories. The top news items were about two high profile murders in Wicomico County: Alice Davis and Sarah Foxwell.

Sarah's story was even more heartbreaking and tragic: she was an eleven-year-old girl who was abducted, sexually assaulted, and murdered by a Salisbury man, Thomas Leggs, Jr. After a three-day search of northern Wicomico County, her body was found on Christmas Day 2009. Her case captured and then broke the hearts of Delmarva residents who could hardly fathom the crime. The news repeatedly showed one particular photograph of Sarah Foxwell. Standing in front of a tree wearing a short-sleeved green button-down shirt, she smiles at the camera revealing a toothy grin, blonde hair trimmed in a neat bob, partially pulled up into a small ponytail. Her eyes are blue. Her arms are tan, as though she spent the summer at the beach or playing in the sun. She is a picture of innocence, stilled forever.

Although the murder happened in 2009, the trial for Thomas Leggs began in March 2011 and was covered extensively by the local media. Leggs ultimately pled guilty and received two life sentences for his horrific crimes. He was sent to a maximum security prison in Western Maryland. A month and a half later, another prisoner slashed him three times in the dining hall with a homemade weapon. Leggs survived the attack.

Just as the coverage of the Sarah Foxwell case dominated the media outlets in early 2011, Alice's story claimed ownership of the late summer headlines. Once again, we struggled to grasp the reality of her murder, the utter cruelty of it. As with Sarah, we were left dumbstruck by the brutality of humanity.

The small stage of Wicomico County's justice system presented familiar faces. Matt Maciarello, who prosecuted Thomas Leggs, Jr., stood shoulder to shoulder with Wicomico County Sheriff Mike Lewis during that terrible week of Alice's disappearance. It was Lewis who said of Sarah Foxwell: "Christmas will never be the same for any of us ever again. I know it won't for me." There was also Davis Ruark. He provided counsel for Sarah's mother, and it was his client who had been stalked and harassed by Jess Davis. In both cases, law enforcement and civilian searchers had combed acres of fields and forests for Sarah and Alice. The public was entreated to come forward with information about them. And, in a horrifying and final turn of events, both Sarah and Alice would be found in the woods, violently murdered and then discarded like trash, left to be forgotten as their remains withered in the natural elements.

Sweet Sarah and beloved Alice.

And, just below their names on that list in *The Daily Times*, the third most popular story was about Hurricane Irene, a storm that had battered the East Coast at the end of August 2011. It first made landfall on the Outer Banks in North Carolina, and made its way to the Delmarva Peninsula on Saturday, August 27th, 2011 — two weeks before Alice's murder. Irene spawned tornadoes in Delaware and left thousands without power. There were widespread reports of damage from high winds and flooding after more than ten inches of rain fell. Families lost their homes; farmers saw fields of corn and tomatoes drowned because the earth, this flat land stuck between a great bay and an ocean, could simply take no more. When Hurricane Irene was finished with Delmarva, she went back to sea. But the storm was not over yet. Irene made a second landfall just outside of Egg Harbor, New Jersey … a place Jess Davis once called home.

Those headlines — Sarah, Alice, Irene — offered up a disheartening summation of 2011. The damage those monsters wrought, the scars on our hearts and upon our land, would not be easily forgotten. If ever.

•   •   •   •   •

Yet Again

In April 2013, about a year a half after Alice's death, my mother asked me to come by her house. She needed help her with her iPad and while closing out her apps, I caught a glimpse of an upcoming event on her calendar: Kidney Biopsy. It caught me by surprise and an old, familiar knot formed in my stomach. Had it come back? Why hadn't she said something to me? How bad was it? Pushing away my frustration and hurt, I fought my instinct to ask her about it. There are two truths I innately understand: the first is I know a kidney biopsy is serious and doesn't happen under normal circumstances, and the second is my mother keeps these sorts of things to herself. So I quickly closed her calendar and said nothing to her.

But as soon as I got in my car, I called my sister to tell her what I'd seen, and just as I anticipated, this was news to Kristen too. We decided we'd let her keep the secret. We both knew it wasn't something she could actually keep from us forever, and that she would tell us, albeit on her timetable. We'd just have to wait for her.

As I drove home, my heart just sank. My mind was an endless loop: *Not again. Please. Not this.*

And Alice. I couldn't help but remember the last time this had happened, when I was just a scared kid in Alice Davis's English class. I couldn't help but remember Alice's kindness and concern. And I couldn't help but remember that Alice was gone now and how her murder broke my heart and how sometimes she appeared in my dreams, causing me such happiness and confusion only to awake in sadness ... Everything was mixed up, all my memories and emotions, the past and the present, and the fear of the future.

The similarities between my mother and Alice were not lost on me. Both women had been loving and nurturing to me; both women had set forward high expectations of me. I wanted to please them and make them proud. But there was something else: the mask. I thought about Alice's stoicism and secrecy, her astounding ability to maintain herself despite the chaos of her world. I thought of my mother keeping her illness from Kristen and me.

Her brave face was intended to save us from fear and worry; she valued strength and resiliency. Alice's mask had failed her; my sister and I also saw right through our mother's pretense.

The biopsy, my mother later revealed to me, proved her worst fears correct. Her kidneys were failing again. After returning from a vacation in Curaçao, she had gone for a routine visit with her nephrologist who promptly informed her that her recent lab results were concerning. She was spilling extremely high amounts of protein in her urine, which is an established benchmark for renal failure. But this time, it was much worse because there was a new diagnosis: focal segmental glomerulosclerosis. The parts of her kidneys that were supposed to filter out waste were turning into scar tissue. It's an uncommon disease, affecting seven people per million or just under 6000 patients in the United States per year. This diagnosis meant my mother went back into treatment to try to stop or slow its process. One doctor prescribed an experimental drug called Acthar. Designed as an anti-inflammation drug, it cost $28,000 per vial and each vial held only a few doses. After only a few rounds of the drug, her condition deteriorated. Her stomach swelled with edema; her skin became too sensitive to touch; and she was in such a constant state of physical pain and nausea that her mind drifted to the darkest of places. Kristen and I were suffused with feelings of anger and outrage, helplessness and fear.

My mother became a medical statistic. A patient in renal failure. Another test tube of blood, another biohazard bottle of urine. Bad lab results followed by worse lab results. It was a Sisyphean fight of pills and insulin, failure and heartbreak. Day after day. Month after month. After two years of trying different drug therapies, nothing had worked and she slipped into Stage Four renal failure. Her doctors who had once floated terms like "dialysis" and "kidney transplant" were now using those words in real time, and in the fall of 2014, my mother was placed on the transplant list. My sister and I were tested to see if we were potential matches. I hoped and I dreamt; I begged the universe to let me be a match.

On December 23rd, 2014, her transplant nurse coordinator from the University of Maryland in Baltimore called me to tell me I was a perfect match. My sister was also a match, but she and our mother had fewer markers in common. When I called my mother, I blurted out the good news and my jubilation was met with complete silence. I waited, unsure of what was coming next. Then there was quiet sobbing. And then: "Stephanie, are you sure about this?"

In my life, I have had absolute certainty about few things, but this decision was instinctual. "Yes," I told her, "I am."

My mother, at first, was not happy about me being her donor. She wanted her new kidney to come from someone else, a stranger who she could thank later. Or thank the family of that stranger. She didn't want my kidney because, as a mother, she didn't want to take anything from her children. Mothers are supposed to give, not take away. So, I devised a scheme. I decided to name my kidneys: Thelma and Louise. Jacki was going to get Louise and I'd keep Thelma. By doing this, we stopped talking about "my kidney." We didn't mention "Stephanie's kidney." From that moment forward, it was Louise and Jacki. Jacki and Louise. It was a silly little trick, but it seemed to help her make some kind of peace with the donation.

There were more rounds of testing for both of us, and she continued to decline. Her kidney function hovered around 28%. It had dipped as low as 13%, but her doctors had been able to adjust her medication. Once my testing was completed, the transplant team met to discuss my folder of test results, and on January 23rd, 2015, the transplant team approved me to donate. Even they were talking about Louise.

Our transplant surgery was scheduled at the University of

Maryland in downtown Baltimore on Monday, March 9th, 2015. The night before, I went to her hotel room to check on her and see how she was doing. Checking on her had become a habit for me, even if she was reticent to talk about her feelings or her condition. She opened the door and I could see she was tired. Just a drive from Salisbury to Baltimore had worn her out. My mother can be a difficult woman to read, but in her eyes, I saw her nervousness. She was anxious and scared. My mother pulled a handwritten note from her suitcase and she burst into tears when she handed it to me. A thank you card. Through her tears, she could only say this: "I just don't know how to thank you for what you're about to do for me."

I pulled her in for a long hug. My fingers found their way to her head again. Small circles. Just as I had done so many years before. Familiar and comforting. This time, though, intended to be so for both of us.

I told her I loved her. She said she loved me too.

The surgery took about eight hours. The doctors removed Louise (my left kidney) along with the vein, artery, and ureter via a single port in my belly button. Louise's new home was in my mother's right lower pelvic region. Her original kidneys were left in place. As soon as Louise was attached, she began making urine. Immediately. It is remarkable how the body just knows what to do. By the time my mother was wheeled into the post-operating recovery area, Louise had made two liters of urine.

Within a month of the kidney transplant, my mother's eyes were no longer swollen and yellow but bright and blue. The edema in her legs and stomach were so drastically reduced that she no longer had rings in her skin just from wearing socks. For the first time in two years, I saw my mother returned to me as the beautiful, strong, and stubborn woman I knew her to be, and I was deeply grateful.

What our family faced, at the beginning, was grim and arduous. We were at the mercy of an aggressive, unsparing disease, and there were times we felt hopeless and distraught. In the darkest times, our family held fast to one another. Love was all we had to give each other. Love and a kidney named Louise.

In the years since the transplant, our journey has proven to be positive in the long run. During those hard years, enduring month after month of watching my mother be ravaged by illness, I often wished I could have called Alice again. How I wished she had been alive so that we may have reconnected. Just the sound of her voice and its gentle, pleasant cadence … her laugh, her humor, her ceaseless kindness. What would she have said to me? What would she have thought of the transplant? Would she have met me for coffee one day and hugged me in the parking lot? I like to think she would have. And in those moments, I came to realize the memory of Alice had to suffice now.

•   •   •   •   •

manie sans délire

In this story of Alice, there is no escaping the gravity of Jess Davis. He was the moon to her earth, pulling her away and moving her in unseen patterns. She was the one swept under the constant tides of humiliation. It was Alice — always Alice, never Jess — who bore the weight of every mistake and awful choice he made. She was invisibly shackled to a life with him, a life from which she could not or would not escape, all because he knew how to play her emotions, because he knew how to push and pull on her heart and her mind.

Because he knew how to break her down.

He embarrassed her. He isolated her. With every lie he told and with every time he let her down, he boxed her in. She maintained a brave face when he robbed her of her dignity by shamelessly parading about in his affairs with younger women. Keeping her marriage together meant enduring his failures, his plots and schemes, his abuse of pain pills, and his inability to just be a good and decent man. Her life with Jess Davis was a hard one and, when she looked for comfort, she found it in the worst possible place: the bottom of a vodka bottle. By the end of her life, her closest friends suspected she was or was on the brink of becoming an alcoholic. As Dawn Neville put it: Alice was drinking volumes.

From the first failed date to her vicious murder, Alice tolerated and then succumbed to the treacherous nature of Jess Davis. *But why?* How did an intelligent, educated woman like Alice not see Jess for what he was? Or if she did, why didn't she leave him?

There was an interesting similarity among many of the women I interviewed. They said Jess was gregarious and convivial, and yet when they heard Alice was missing, they immediately suspected he had something to do with it. This struck me as unusual at first. How do these two things reconcile? And then the answer came to me as I stared at a photograph of Jess Davis — it was the mask, his mask. It is the Jekyll and Hyde we have come to know.

Jess had the ability to be socially agreeable, funny, helpful even. Once, in church he handed the preacher fifty dollars to give to a needy parishioner. (He said he felt compelled to give, something was calling him, telling him to do it.) Another time, after a big snow storm, he drove across the county to plow the driveway for an elderly lady he knew. The friendships he made with men like Matthew Collier were decades long. And there were the genuinely sweet relationships he had with Colleen Dallam's boys and Lori's children, especially his grandson. These glimpses into the tender-hearted paternal side of Jess contrast greatly against the specters of his own father and stepfather, two figures who loomed silently in his background. If nature and nuture are two halves of the same coin, then the conflicts within Jess Davis are even more painfully clear.

Alice found him charming, unlike anyone she had ever met and certainly unlike anyone she had ever allowed to be close to her. He made her laugh. He made her feel loved and desired, and in turn she loved him. He made her believe he needed her and her alone, that only Alice could save him and protect him, that only Alice could see what so many others could not because she was different, which in turn made him the luckiest man alive. This need, this desire — it was a powerful elixir. And so Alice made concessions. He would never be like the men her sister's husbands were. He would never be like the men her teacher friends had married. He would never be Romeo, but he would be hers for better or worse.

Yet when his mask slipped, the charm transformed into viciousness. The reality was much more stark than she recognized. In truth, Alice had been conned. He had her. He weaponized her vulnerability and her intelligence against herself. All of it — the need, the desire, the love — all of it was a ruse. She was sucked into the vacuum of his personality, a black hole of narcissism and deceit, and she never returned.

Jess is the villian in this story. I have often wondered if understanding him could or would shed any light on what happened to Alice. Then, one night, I was driving home and listening to an episode of the *Criminal* podcast. It was about a woman named Axton Betz-Hamilton whose mother had stolen her identity and taken out credit cards in her name. Axton's life and most definitely her credit score had been nearly ruined by her mother who had lied and manipulated her. The stolen identity was a heartbreaking facet to her story, but it was the discussion about psychopathy that fascinated me the most.

In that episode, Jon Ronson, British journalist and author of *The Psychopath Test*, spoke about a check list for those listeners curious to see if they or someone they loved had it. The twenty-point list was created by Dr. Robert Hare for mental health professionals, and each item is scored from 0 to 2, depending how present the trait is. A score above 30 is indicative of a psychopathic mind. For scale, Ted Bundy got a 39 out of 40.

The twenty items were: glib and superficial charm, grandiose estimation of self, need for stimulation, pathological lying, cunning and manipulativeness, lack of remorse or guilt, shallow affect, callousness and lack of empathy, parasitic lifestyle, poor behavioral controls, sexual promiscuity, early behavior problems, lack of realistic long-term goals, impulsivity, irresponsibility, failure to accept responsibility for one's actions, many short-term marital relationships, juvenile delinquency, revocation of conditional release, and criminal versatility.

I listened to each bullet point and wondered, *what if Jess Davis was a psychopath or sociopath or had some of those traits? What does that mean? And does it help me understand what happened to Alice?*

• • • • •

Ancient Greek thinker Theophrastus, a successor of Aristotle, reportedly wrote a volume called *Characters* on the various types of moral characters. He put forward The Unscrupulous Man: "The Unscrupulous Man will go and borrow more money from a creditor he has never paid ... When marketing he reminds the butcher of some service he has rendered him and, standing near the scales, throws in some meat, if he can, and a soup-bone. If he succeeds, so much the better; if not, he will snatch a piece of tripe and go off laughing." Here, Theophrastus gave us one of the earliest portrayals of a sociopath — *a conscienceless human,* a person who knows right from wrong and chooses wrong without compunction and without hesitation. An 18th century French physician named Philippe Pinel, who worked with psychiatric patients, put forward the term "manie sans délire" or loosely translated as "insanity without delusion." Look at the man in Theophrastus' example who gleefully cheats the butcher without a scintilla of remorse. Pinel had patients who exhibited maniacal behaviors but did so without hallucinations or delusions of grandeur or flights of fantasy. Herein lies a quandary: what do we make of a person who is intellectually aware of right and wrong and yet who choses to do wrong, remaining completely unencumbered by conscience?

Simply saying the word "sociopath" or "psychopath" conjures up powerful images: Hollywood gave us the likes of Hannibal Lecter, Norman Bates, and Dexter, while real life terrified us with Charles Manson, Jeffrey Dahmer, and David Berkowitz. We have sensationalized these words in our modern culture: look at any slasher movie or listen to true crime podcasts. But what do they mean? We often use these words interchangeably, and we are wrong when we do. One arguable distinction is that the psychopath is higher functioning, more intellectually sophisticated, and devoid of forming bonds with others whereas a sociopath is often more erratic, less cultivated, yet able to form some relationships with those around them.

The modern medical and psychology communities are hestitant to label a person as a psychopath or a sociopath, but rather they use the term "antisocial personality disorder." Mental health professionals use the Diagnostic and Statistical Manual of Mental Disorders when making a determination about a patient's possible antisocial personality disorder. The diagnosis *can be considered* if the patient exhibits three or more of the following seven traits:

- Failure to conform to social norms with respect to lawful behaviors (as indicated by repeatedly performing acts that are grounds for arrest)
- Deceitfulness, as indicated by repeated lying, use of aliases or conning others for personal profit or pleasure
- Impulsivity, failure to plan ahead
- Irritability and aggressiveness (as indicated by repeated physical fights or assaults)
- Feckless disregard for safety of self or others
- Consistent irresponsibility as indicated by repeated failure to sustain consistent work behavior or honor financial obligations
- Lack of remorse as indicated by being indifferent to or rationalizing having hurt, mistreated, or stolen from another

This is the kind of information that shocks the system. It is the kind of information that makes you take stock of the people in your life — past, present, and future — because we all know someone who nails several of those bullets points. In my research, I found Martha Stout's book, *The Sociopath Next Door*. Just below the title on the cover of the book is this staggering statistic: "1 in 25 ordinary Americans secretly has no conscience and can do anything at all without feeling guilty." If she's right, then a lot of things that go wrong start to make sense.

Stout emphasizes that simply having an antisocial personality disorder does not automatically equate to criminality. Someone with antisocial personality disorder can be a killer, but they can just as easily be a frail, silver-haired grandmother who subjects her family to decades of verbal, mental, and emotional abuse, or a company CEO who berates and fires employees on a whim and fails to pay on contractual obligations so that he can pocket the corporate profits. Think about the childhood bully who laughs while tormenting children or animals. Murder is not a necessary ingredient; the guiltlessness is. That is the key. Having said that, Stout maintains the likelihood of a person with antisocial personality disorder committing a crime is greater, given that one of the key features is the lack of remorse for their actions.

I had to digest this concept that there are people among us who just never feel guilt or shame or remorse. Think of the freedom they must feel. Put yourself here for a moment: without a personal conviction to guide you, without a respect for social rules or laws to keep you in check, without a conscience, what would you do? It would be like having a superpower. You could do anything you wanted and still fall asleep with the ease of a newborn baby. If you knew it wouldn't bother you, why wouldn't you lie and cheat? Outside of the threat of being caught, why wouldn't you rob a bank? Or kill your wife?

The concept of the psychopath/sociopath is shattering because it challenges our senses of good and evil, of right and wrong, and of equity and morality. How can a person commit horrific crimes and not feel guilt or remorse or shame? And if they cannot feel such things, then how do we punish them? How can we know justice or peace? In the collective social mind, we want people to feel badly for what they have done because it helps us feel as though the scales are balancing. It makes us feel better. But these people change all that. In recent years, some states like Oklahoma have changed their position on allowing defendants with antisocial personality disorders to use insanity pleas. While the crimes may seem insane, they understood right from wrong and made a choice, and because these defendants have no ability to feel remorse, the legal system is faced with a greater problem — the risk of another offense. This is not to say Oklahoma has a perfect grasp on it. These defendants are complicated, and often, the legal system and the mental health professionals can be at odds, especially given that new research is showing *possible* links between certain brain deformities and anti-social personality disorder. This brings up the eternal question of nature versus nuture: are people born this way or are they made? Plainly, the answer maybe both. While the law and the government demand black and white answers, the world of psychiatrists and psychologists see many shades of gray because, if nothing else, so-ciopaths can be exceptionally complex.

And they are everywhere, according to Martha Stout. She believes the rate of sociopathy in our society is as high as 4%, which means we are more likely to know a psychopath/sociopath than to know someone with colon cancer or schizophrenia. Think of it this way: 4% of the United States population roughly translates into *13 million people. Yes. Millions of psychopaths and sociopaths.* Just walking among us. In our workplaces. In our neighborhoods. In our families.

Their camouflage involves wearing a mask, one they have crafted over years of watching others. Psychopaths and sociopaths can be absolutely charming, and this duality is part of their danger. In order to get what they want from society and to get what they want from the people around them, they often learn how to imitate con-scientious behavior and personal responsibility. This builds trust and connections, which can then be exploited once they figure out the rules and constructs. The game is always on and it can escalate in an instant.

We tend to think of the havoc psychopaths and sociopaths wreak on society in the largest magnitudes: murders, rapes, kid-napping, mass casualty assaults, even white collar crimes like Ponzi schemes and Wall Street frauds, but there is an entire universe to fill with the damage they inflict on a smaller scale. There are spouses, family members, and friends who suffer the lasting effects of physical, sexual, verbal, mental, emotional, and financial abuse at the hands of people with antisocial personality disorder. The damage is real and long-term. Victims may turn to counseling, or they may turn to a number of unhealthy alternatives such as alcohol, drugs, self-harm, obsessive and compulsive behaviors, or even suicide, all to medicate the pain, which often spins off an entirely new cycle of dysfunction. The damage can be generational, passed down like a toxic heirloom. Victims are the ones left with a deep sense of shame, guilt, and remorse, which is perhaps one of the cruelest and most ironic twists.

But if we knew and understood how psychopaths and sociopaths operate, would we be able to see our own tormentors differently? Would we be able to sever ties with them?

Would we be able to survive them?

There is no public information, documentation, or testimony to prove or acknowledge or even hint that Jess Henry Davis, Jr. had any psychological diagnosis at all. There was nothing of the sort mentioned in the police records. Some of his medical history can be pieced together through his list of prescriptions. There were medications for diabetes, pain management, high blood pressure, thyroid issues, and erectile dysfunction, but there was nothing to suggest treatment for mental health. Alice, on the other hand, was on a low dose of an antidepressant. It was in her list of prescriptions and it was also present in the post-mortem toxicology report. I am not a mental health professional and I do not hold any degrees or certifications in this field. However, there is clear and accessible research that outlines the behaviors and personality traits of people with antisocial personality disorders, and reading these descriptions with Jess Davis in mind has been incredibly enlightening for me.

In my conversations with family and friends as well as my interviews with police, I tried to capture their sense of Jess Davis. How did they perceive him? *What was he like?* As the stories unfolded, with each detail and anecdote assembled before me, an unflattering picture began to form: someone sly and dangerous concealed behind the mask of an over-the-top, good old boy. I began thinking back on all the stories about Jess Davis, the things he did and said, the person he was. I listed every point on a sheet of paper and the laundry list began.

For example, there was a story Marisa and Maria told me about how Jess laughed and smiled when he told them about watching a movie called *Faces of Death*. The film was banned in several countries due to its specific and graphic nature including scenes (some fake, some real) of human death and even animal torture. Marisa was repulsed by Jess's belly laughs over it and the moment left her thinking, *he actually enjoyed that movie.* The very idea that death, torture, and murder were funny or benign to him shines a light on his darkness.

There was also a little anecdote I found in the police files. In the month before the murder, Jess sold his pickup for $4,300; during the sale, he told the buyer that he was a sniper and a former NJ State Trooper. Neither of those things was true. He didn't need to lie to the buyer, but he did anyway. For no purpose or gain. Just to do it. It looks bizarre at best and pathological at worse. And six months before the murder, the Department of Natural Resources Police filed charges against him for operating his taxidermy business without a license. As a longtime hunter and taxidermist, it is inconceivable to think he would not have known he'd need the proper licensing. This was just one more illustration of his defiance of the law, of order, of doing the things expected of every one else. But rules didn't apply to him.

When I was finished with this Jess Davis laundry list, I found myself staring at a portrait of a man who nailed just about every criterion in the DSM for antisocial personality disorder.

But if the hallmark of that diagnosis is a lack of remorse, then the greatest and most revealing evidence against Jess Davis is this: Detective Metzger watched Jess "cry" without any tears coming from his eyes. People on the phone with him felt that he was faking his emotions, indicating that he would be crying one minute, then talking normally, then crying again. The disconnect between his words and his tone: he said he was worried about Alice but he could not manufacture any sincerity in his voice. When Detective Blades questioned him in the police car, Jess spoke of his concerns for himself and the cats, but not Alice. *Never Alice.* Even in his last words — the suicide note — he shifted all the blame onto the police. There was no morsel of shame or guilt for what he had done. He never accepted responsibility for any of it.

In the end, the most shocking and telling piece of this puzzle is Jess Davis's absolute lack of remorse for his worst offense — the murder of Alice, his wife of 26 years, the woman who loved him, even when it was too late.

•　•　•　•　•

"... as men in rage strike those that wish them best ..."

Shakespeare wrote *Othello* in 1603. It is a play in which a husband, a masculine and virile character with a violent past, murders his kind and submissive wife in a jealous and furious rage. Othello laments that he loved not well, but *too much* as Desdemona lies strangled in their matrimonial bed, forever silenced in her obedience and her love of a dangerous man. Othello's final act is suicide — violence against himself. When Emilia reveals her husband Iago as the catalyst and instigator for Othello's actions, the consequence is deadly: Iago kills her too. Dead wives are often the denouement for angry and conniving husbands. Whether they quietly maintain their positions or bravely speak out, the women of *Othello* die at the hands of their lovers, their protectors, their husbands. This is an irony that will not be lost on those who knew and loved Alice Davis.

In 2011, the year Alice was murdered, there were more than 1,700 American women murdered by men in single victim/single offender situations. Of those women, 1,509 knew their killers, and of those, at least 926 women were the wives or intimate partners of their killers. Most of these women were shot. And while South Carolina was the deadliest state for women in 2011, Maryland was ranked 18th; Alice was one of 40 women killed in single victim/single offender homicide in that year.

Although Hollywood likes to scare its audiences with movies and television shows about serial killers and stalkers and strangers torturing women snatched from parking lots and darkened bedrooms, the reality is always much closer to home. Women are far more likely to be harmed by someone they know, by someone they love. Even our celebrities and entertainment idols cross the lines. In 2011, actor Nicholas Cage reportedly grabbed his wife in the streets of New Orleans and began punching vehicles before he was stopped and arrested by police. In November 2011, actor Gary Dourdan from the CBS hit drama *CSI*, broke his girlfriend's nose and was arrested for felony battery. What is striking is that both Cage and Dourdan have played roles of sensitive, tender men — men who safeguard others from the harms and threats of the world.

Shakespeare was right: everything is a mask.

The number of stories about women harmed and murdered by the men who were supposed to love and protect them is incalculable. In most cases, there are warning signs along the way:

possessiveness, isolation, threats, controlling behaviors, a quick temper, and brutality. Patterns emerge. Tranquil seas give way to unexpected squalls followed by hurricanes which fade into the distance as a static-filled calm fills the void. Repeat. Repeat. *Repeat.*

Domestic violence knows no barriers. It happens to women and men of every race, religion, nationality, and socio-economic background. The statistics are shocking: 1 in 4 women and 1 in 9 men experience domestic violence, which includes physical and sexual violence as well as stalking. The National Coalition Against Domestic Violence identifies domestic violence as "the willful intimidation, physical assault, battery, sexual assault, and/or other abusive behavior as part of a systematic pattern of power and control perpetrated by one intimate partner against another. It includes physical violence, sexual violence, threats, and emotional abuse. The frequency and severity of domestic violence can vary dramatically." TheHotline.org, the website for the National Domestic Violence Hotline, sums it up a little more succinctly as "a pattern of behaviors used by one partner to maintain power and control over another partner in an intimate relationship."

In simplest terms: Alice may not have thought her relationship with Jess was abusive, especially if he never hit her. We often think of physical violence as the primary telltale sign, but given what is now known about their relationship and about Jess, their relationship had markers of abuse. He isolated a shy, naive woman. He drained her financially, limiting her resources and ability to leave had she chosen to do so. He manipulated her with flattery. He lied to her. He cheated on her. He was dishonest and disrespectful. He assaulted her family members and threatened to kill his own. He was intimidating and was sexually inappropriate with other women. He kept her world small, likely filling what remained with shame, embarrassment, and guilt because he knew it would keep her in place.

And then he killed her.

Was Jess physically abusive to Alice? Colleen Dallam *thought* she saw a bruise on Alice's forearm the month before the murder. But was it actually there? And even if it was, did it result from an encounter with Jess? Dawn saw bruises on Alice but Alice attributed those to her drinking. If abuse is a learned behavior, then Jess had ample opportunity to learn from his father and stepfather, and if abuse escalates with the use of drugs and alcohol, then his penchant for drinking and pain pills were the proverbial gasoline on an open fire. The truth is we don't know if he was physically violent with her and we won't ever know that. Or if someone does, they have kept her secrets.

Is it possible that he first laid angry hands on her when he killed her? Yes, it is possible. Such a thing is not unheard of. For example, consider the case of Laura Wallen, who was four months pregnant in Montgomery County, Maryland in early September 2017. Her fiancé, Tyler Tessier, shot her in the back of head after she discovered that he was having an affair with another woman. Wallen, a social studies teacher, failed to report to school, which kicked off a massive search for her. She was found in a heavily wooded area off Prices Distillery Road in Damascus, Maryland. Tessier was arrested for her murder and he later committed suicide in his prison cell on the day his trial was to start. According to newspaper accounts, there was no indication of previous abuse or a volatile relationship between them. No reports of 911 calls or fights or protective orders. Her family, who did not like Tessier, did not know of any physical abuse occuring in their relationship. It appears as though the first sign of his violence was her murder.

Just the same as Desdemona with Othello.

Just the same as Alice with Jess.

This is crucial to understand. A lover can kill without ever before having shown a dangerous hand. Alice is not alone. Despite the shock and horror of her murder, it is not unusual. Time and time again, as I have worked on Alice's story, people have asked me, "What about the husband? Were there any warning signs?" Looking back on their history together, the red flags are visible and clear — his lying, his cheating, his stealing, his threats, his aggression, his control — but for all his machinations, Alice did not seem afraid of him. She had once said, "Jess wouldn't hurt a hair on my head."

Perhaps Alice never thought he would turn on her. She was wrong. Her story ended abruptly and violently. Her story ended in sadness and statistics. Maybe Alice didn't know the different signs of domestic violence. Or maybe she did. Maybe she saw the signs and willed herself into a stoic state of denial. Maybe she resigned herself to whatever life she had because she thought she couldn't do better.

But we *know* better.

And yet, in the heartbreak of it, here is one of the greatest chances for her story to mean something. Her tragic end has the potential to change the storyline of other women. Could Alice's story be a light in the darkness for someone else? What if someone recognized the warnings signs in Jess's behavior? What if one person learns about Alice — who she was, what happened to her, how she still means something to the ones she left behind — and what if that one person makes a change?

What if Alice's story rewrites an ending for someone else?

Part V

*"Love all,
trust a few,
do wrong to none."*

ALL'S WELL THAT ENDS WELL
ACT I, SCENE i

The Sum of Our Scars

Trauma is often spoken of like a wound, a raw gaping hole finally stitched over, scarred and forever sealed into the limb or body. As the months and years pass over us like so many waves upon a shoreline, those rips in our flesh are rendered as smooth as river rocks as we bend and yield to the marches of time. The purple bruises and pink scars remind us of the horrible and the accidental, the cruel and the unusual. We may be considered whole, but we are merely mended on the outside.

But trauma is more insidious. It roots down inside of us. It snakes around our internal organs, fastening itself to our muscles and bones, swimming along invisibly in our blood. Every cell, every raw thing within us becomes ensnared in the relentlessness of the unspeakable. Soldiers holding bits and pieces of their comrades. Young girls living with men who enter their bedrooms at night. The spouse of a World Trade Center worker. Rape victims. Battered wives. The elderly neighbor with a number tattooed on a forearm.

Whether accrued in a single horrific incident or acquired over a lifetime, the rooting of trauma changes us from the inside out. It can disrupt our sleep patterns and cause ulcers. Our brains often form obsessive and compulsive thought patterns as a coping mechanism. Anxiety and doubt leach us of self-esteem, feeding on it for sustenance and draining us of confidence. We begin to pull inward. We begin to build defenses.

The trauma of a childhood illness surely changed young Alice. Imagine her as a little girl, sensitive and shy by nature, waking up on the classroom floor surrounded by her schoolmates with no recollection as to how she got there. The loss of consciousness and her bodily functions had to be utterly embarrassing and mortifying for a young girl. These events happened to her again and again and again. The repetitive nature of her childhood epilepsy should not be overlooked and cannot be emphasized enough in understanding how Alice's defense mechanisms began to build … the foundations upon which she would build her walls. This sense of being different formed early and became a framework for how she would see herself in the world. In high school, she made fun of the "clique kids" to make herself feel better, and making fun of them with Gale meant she wasn't alone. As a young woman, she left Washington, D.C. and returned to Allen because she felt she didn't belong there. Alice came home not because she wasn't smart enough but because she wasn't sure enough.

And there were men in her life who reinforced, either accidentally or purposefully, this timorous internal framework. The unfortunate and unintentional reinforcement from Casey started early. He worried and fretted over her because of the epilepsy; he overprotected out of love. Casey understood the world could be a dark place — he had seen what cruelty could do. Childhood to adulthood, he remained an overshadowing figure. If Alice fell down, Casey picked her up. If Alice needed money, Casey emptied his wallet. She was forever his wounded sparrow and required his protection, which he gave again and again. But in his safekeeping, he handicapped her because Alice was unable to distinguish the very real difference between being under her father's wing and being under her husband's thumb.

Perhaps unconsciously Alice believed love was supposed to be omnipresent, always there and always looming like dense fog caught in a valley. There is no question Casey loved his children. There is no question Casey was a good man doing what he believed was best. And it is woeful upon regrettable that their dynamic rendered her susceptible to the charms and ills of Jess Henry Davis, Jr.

Alice mistook her husband's intensity for love. To her, his

needful nature was simply a byproduct of a troubled childhood, something to which she could relate. She could nurture him, give him the reassurance Casey had given her. He was a feral creature who revealed and subjected himself to her and her alone. If he was loud and brash, it was because he needed to be understood. Only Alice could see him, truly see him. Her family didn't get him, but because Alice knew what being different felt like, she acted as both his interpreter and his champion.

But love is not supposed to hurt. Love is not supposed to suffocate or isolate or push down. Love never wears the mask of manipulation.

The connection between her chronic childhood epilepsy and her father's overprotection influenced and shaped who Alice would become. And while it made her vulnerable to Jess Davis, it also engendered in her a keen sensitivity. Alice had a sixth sense for struggling children. She was emboldened to reach out and connect with her students in a way other teachers could not or would not. She saw the ones who were hurting, the ones who were different, the ones who were struggling and searching. Sensitivity was second nature to her, honed over time and through her own suffering. It is how she saw me. She knew there was more to my story; she knew there was more to it than just a silly high school senior blowing off an assignment. Alice sensed my heartache and gave me the only thing she had: *she gave herself.*

And this is the duality of trauma. It renders us irrevocably changed and vulnerable while also making us more attuned to the vibrations of others around us. It makes us build walls around ourselves and yet makes us extend our hearts and our hands to kindred spirits. Trauma narrates our stories, but in the telling, we become something greater, something more than the sum of our scars.

• • • • •

"I hope to tell you."

There remains little mystery as to what happened to Alice. Almost as quickly as she had been declared a missing person, she was declared dead and her case was closed. She wasn't lost anymore, no longer simply out there somewhere. The reporters spoke her name one last time and moved on to new stories. The police put away their files and focused their attention on new crimes. The hammers they took into evidence were never tested. There was no need. The case was closed. The Wicomico County Bureau of Investigations, the team of law enforcement officers responsible for Alice's case, disbanded in 2016. Sheriff Mike Lewis remains in charge of the Wicomico County Sheriff's Department and will likely be for the foreseeable future. He won his initial election in a relative landslide in 2006 and has since run unopposed for three more terms. Matthew Maciarello, the state's attorney who sat at Lewis's side during press conferences about Alice Davis, is now a judge in the Wicomico County Circuit Court. One of Alice's students, Jamie Dykes, replaced Maciarello as the new state's attorney in 2018, the first woman to be elected to that position.

For the ones she left behind, healing has been somewhere in the middle distance. When the shock and horror were still fresh, forgiveness and contented reflection felt light-years away. The tragic loss of Alice meant her family, friends, and students had to face the gauntlet of emotions and memories that come with having known and loved someone who was murdered. It is unlike losing someone to cancer or a car wreck: we understand illness and we can grasp that accidents happen. We can assimilate those as terrible yet normal facts of life. Murder is different. No matter how much we see it on television, once it takes someone you know, someone you love, one truth becomes crystal clear: you will never be indifferent to it again. Every time you hear a story like Alice's, you will think of the one you lost.

• • • • •

For Barrie Tilghman and Ellen Hitch and their families, the healing started with their faith and with each other. They miss their little sister. A piece of their family has been cleaved off. Family photographs always present a reminder of their losses: Mary Belle, Casey, and Alice. Now the three of them lie together in the cemetery at the little Methodist church in Allen with the cedar trees and centuries old gravestones. When Barrie and Ellen speak of Alice, there are always notes of regret and sorrow in their voices underpinning even the more lighthearted and happier memories. They wish Jess Davis had never come along. They wish Alice had had better judgement when it came to him. She could see everyone else so clearly … why not him? Theirs is a frustration they can do nothing with except try to let it go.

Barrie and Ellen have made peace with their heartache and the relationship they had with Alice. Sisterhood is a marvel: it can be tender and adoring and it can also be troubled and vexing. No one is perfect — any woman with a sister will tell you that. The Parsons girls were brought up in the Methodist faith and Barrie and Ellen remain strong in their Christian beliefs. Two of the big tenants are love and forgiveness. Moving forward for them has meant just that, and putting their faith in God. They may not have fully understood Alice's story but they believe there is a higher purpose in it.

Their families have sought to honor Alice's memory, each one in their own way. Ellen and Scott's grandson, Alex, tattooed her date of death on his shoulder. Barrie and Ellen established a scholarship fund in Alice's name that is held at the Community Foundation of the Eastern Shore. The Alice Parsons Davis Memorial Scholarship is a $500 award given to an applicant in Wicomico County who is headed to a two-year or four-year institution to study English, Journalism, Creative Writing or History. And in keeping with Alice's way of teaching, the winning student must have a 4.0 GPA, be of good character, and complete a 40-minute timed essay developed by an AP English or History teacher.

And there is Lori Lopez. She lost more than anyone else. She lost Alice and Jess. She saw her children lose a grandmother and a grandfather just a few years after the death of their brother. The grief and the losses she has suffered in her life are unimaginable. Yet she rose each and every day to face it: she met with Sheriff Lewis and the detectives to see how she could help; she and Johnny scrubbed the floor where Jess's blood had congealed onto the hard wood; and she acquiesced to Barrie's wishes that she stay away.

After Jess committed suicide, Lori sat with her mother and the two women wept as they talked. At first it was the shock of the events, but then it began to occur to Lori that they were crying for another reason altogether. These were tears of relief. Her mother was the one who gave voice to it: "After all this time, I don't have to look over my shoulder anymore."

Lori spread Jess Henry Davis Jr.'s ashes in a spot where he often went hunting in Maryland. She visited Alice's graveside after the tension of the funeral passed. She still visits.

In the years since the deaths of her son and Alice and Jess, Lori has become a beacon of hope for her community in New Jersey. People see her as someone who understands tragic loss and, perhaps most importantly, as someone who understands how to overcome terrible obstacles. When her daughter's friend was killed in a car crash, they turned to Lori for guidance and support. She had navigated this before — they hadn't. They leaned on her. When a friend was diagnosed with terminal brain cancer, Lori arranged a "beef and beer" fundraiser, which garnered more than $10,000 to help with hospital bills. Lori seems to hold the secret: one day at a time, one minute at a time. Breathe in and breathe out. One foot in front of the other. Again and again. Until you are on the other side of the panic and the pain.

The only way to get there is forward.

•　•　•　•　•　•

Gale Glasgow Dashiell still loves the little girl who had befriended her all those years ago. Despite the distance and awkwardness between them as grown woman, Alice will always and forever be her childhood best friend. Nothing can or will erase that. Every time Gale hears one of those old songs by Elton John or Carol King or The Beatles, she thinks of teenaged Alice, singing and smiling, contented and happy. Pink carnations and "American Pie." She prefers to remember Alice in those better moments. Whether walking through the woods of Allen with pockets full of candy or stealing whiskey from the Parsons's liquor cabin, Gale holds fast to the memories that bring Alice into full focus, alive and happy and full of possibility. Like the time when she went over to Alice's house for New Year's Eve; Gale, Alice, and Alice's cousins, Leslie and Cliff, sneaked into the old Methodist church in Allen and raced up the steeple. The quiet of the cold night was shattered when all four of them grabbed the rope and rang the bell with all their might, exuberant and laughing. Gale likes to think of how, when Alice was excited and bursting with anticipation or happiness, she'd say,

"I hope to tell you!" The silly little phrase always made Gale laugh because the only other person she'd ever heard say that was Barney Fife on *The Andy Griffith Show*. Now, all these decades later, that peculiar exclamation spoke to Gale differently: it made her think of Alice's innocence, her sweet and good-natured way of moving through the world even when it was hardest on her.

On the one-year anniversary of her death, Marisa and Maria, Alice and Jess's old neighbors, arranged to have a memorial sign posted in Allen. It was a small token of remembrance in their village where a number of ugly rumors about Jess continued to swirl. In one, Casey Parsons allegedly told a lady confidante that he thought Jess had killed his dog. She had been fine in the morning and Casey came home to find her dead in the front yard. There was no clear or obvious reason for it. Another rumor suggested that Alice may not have been his first victim. As that particular story goes, Jess did handyman work for an elderly woman on Perryhawkin Road in Princess Anne who drowned in a bathtub. Her coin collection went missing, and not long afterward, Jess bought a new truck. There was also an allegation that he was involved in an illegal marijuana growing operation somewhere in the forests around Wicomico County. As the rumors came and went, Marisa and Maria often wondered if any of them were true. But then again, there was no one to dispute them anymore.

For Matthew Collier, the months and years since the deaths of his friends have brought little in the way of reconciliation. Jess had been his dear friend for nearly 30 years. They hunted together, helped each other in times of need, and spent holidays together. Matthew felt like he had been spun around and around. He and his family had spent the July 4th holiday with Jess and Alice just two months before the murder and everything seemed fine. There wasn't a single thing about Jess — not a comment, not a look, not a vibe — to suggest the tragedy ahead. What does a person do when someone they love does something completely unfathomable? Does that negate all the good? Matthew Collier still struggles with that. He struggles to reconcile the Jeckyl and Hyde of Jess Davis: the Jess he knew and the Jess who murdered Alice. He is left holding onto good memories of Jess and Alice as well as the heartbreak of their deaths.

•   •   •   •   •

After we came together to honor Alice at the memorial service and again at her funeral, as much as it hurt, we all turned our eyes toward the road ahead. We had to. We could not live there in the past anymore. We were all changed. No one was better for having gone through it. Instead, we were all broken. Tiny cracks in our own masks. Tears and anger. Brave hearts faltering. But perhaps the real work of healing is to become stronger in those broken places … to seal the fissures and fractures with laughter and good works, with warm memories and living our lives in ways which will pay tribute to the light she saw in each of us.

The sisterhood of Parkside teachers has changed. They no longer get together for lunches in the summer. After Alice died, a piece was missing. It made for stilted conversation and awkward silences. Each of them was left with confusion and frustration, regret and guilt, anger and heartache over what had happened to Alice. How could he do that to her? How bad had it been? What clue had they missed? And perhaps the most agonizing question of all: why hadn't Alice reached out to one of them?

But the distance wasn't just the result of Alice's death. They were also getting older, moving away, caring for ailing spouses or energetic grandchildren. Some of them were retiring from teaching while some assumed new professional roles. Life was simply moving them in different directions.

They remember Alice in personal moments. Colleen Dallam has a picture of Alice. In it, she's wearing a scarf and it makes Colleen smile because it reminds her of a joke among the teachers. The entire English department wore scarves except for Alice so they decided to get her one. Alice laughed about it, but she wore the scarf — a subtle symbol of her belonging. She thinks of Alice during the holidays, when Alice and Jess invited her and her young boys to spend Thanksgivings and Christmases with them. They opened their homes and their hearts, and that is a kindness Colleen will never forget.

Cindy Bennett thinks of Alice every Christmas because each year Alice gave her a White House ornament. She remembers her sense of humor and her laugh, which is often followed by thinking about how Alice hid all the bad things in her life behind her smiles and dry quips. Often, Cindy wishes she could hear Alice's laugh again.

Dawn Neville watched Alice grow up, from Alice Parsons with large, wire-rimmed glasses and her long, brown hair parted down the middle in Dawn's homeroom class at Bennett Senior High School to Alice Davis, the enthusiastic yet by-the-book teacher and eventual chair of the English Department. It was an enormous transition, a point of bittersweet reflection for Dawn.

Anne Collins remembers her every year when the senior awards are due. Alice used to sit on the scholarship committee that Anne created in her parents' name; when that seat became empty, Anne reached out to one of Alice's former students as a replacement. She needed someone to read the essays and look for the qualities Alice might have. (That former student? Me.)

Aimee Yeingst is now Aimee Orme and the 2019-2020 school year marked her 23rd at Parkside High School. When she looks around the halls now, she recognizes there are only a few teachers who remember Alice Davis and when they leave, that last connection will be gone forever. It's bittersweet. Alice was Aimee's teaching mentor, second mother, and dear friend and Aimee still misses her. As she puts it: there's always going to be a hole in her heart for Alice.

Micah Stauffer left Parkside High School in 2014 and is now the Chief Finance and Operations Officer for the Wicomico County Board of Education. It's a long way from being a first year science teacher. During his five years as principal, he helped navigate his students and faculty through several traumatic events, beginning with Alice's death. He remembers how he counted on his faith to help him be a leader in a time of crisis ... to walk with integrity, to be hopeful yet honest. The weeks were hard, but with the support of the teaching staff, they all made it through the year. At the 2011-2012 graduation ceremony, Micah Stauffer, along with the rest of the staff, wore green and white ribbons in honor of Alice Davis. And everyone took a moment of silence to remember her.

• • • • • •

In May 2013, the Dalai Lama wrote, "Just as ripples spread out when a single pebble is dropped into water, the actions of individuals can have far-reaching effects." This is how I think of Alice's impact now.

Her classroom was a launch pad for future lawyers and federal prosecutors, journalists and authors, teachers and coaches. She had a hand in helping a future Associated Press editor get into the right English class after being incorrectly placed by the school administrative office. Year after year, dozens and dozens of students would file out of her classroom door, bound for bigger and better things.

Many of them would look back and credit her with pushing them and presenting them with a simple rule: use no one but yourself as a yardstick for measuring your success.

Alice only ever asked us to better ourselves, to see what else we could accomplish. Find spots where we can tighten up a sentence or dig deeper into a story. Every time I use passive voice in my writing, Alice comes into my mind, giving a "tsk tsk" and I rearrange the words on the page. Alice urged us to find the lesson in a story. Let it mean something and carry it forward.

All these years later, her voice still echoes with us. Something special remains. The lives she touched continue to move forward in this world and that can never be undone.

We are her legacy now.

Dixie White walked into Alice Parson's classroom as a freshman in September 1983. Although Dixie had dreams of being a pharmacist, she had always loved English, and right away, Ms. Parsons made her feel comfortable and eager to learn. Ms. Parsons was a new, first-year teacher and it showed: Ms. Parsons didn't exactly rule her class so much as she was just so nice to everyone. No hints of sternness or a closed fist. Her warmhearted nature helped all the students to feel at ease, especially during the journaling portions of the course work which often required reading and speaking in front of the class. Because they felt comfortable with Ms. Parsons, the task of public speaking became easier, less frightening. Having Ms. Parsons was a gentle place for Dixie and the other nervous freshman to springboard into their high school careers.

In the summer months before her junior year, Dixie received her class schedule in the mail. She was hoping to get Ms. Parsons again for her English class, but her heart fell when she saw another name instead: Mrs. Davis.

"Who is Mrs. Davis?" Dixie grumbled. Her disappointment was short-lived, however, when she walked into the classroom and saw Ms. Parsons standing by her desk. Once they were settled, Mrs. Davis, with a radiant smile, told the class about her summer wedding. Dixie was delighted on two fronts: first, she had the teacher she had wanted, and second, Mrs. Davis was really happy about her marriage.

High school isn't always a great experience for teenagers and Dixie was no exception. She had a lot going on at home, making her all the more aware of Mrs. Davis's kindness and support. When Dixie doubted herself, there was Mrs. Davis telling her she could do anything she set her mind to; when Dixie felt low, Mrs. Davis was right there telling her she had value. Coming from another teacher, she might have blown off the sentiments, but Mrs. Davis had a way of speaking to Dixie, *a way of reaching* Dixie, which made her feel those things were true. Dixie believed in herself because Mrs. Davis believed in her. That, more than anything, was one of the greatest lessons Dixie learned in Mrs. Davis's classroom.

Dixie White Leikach became a pharmacist. She has lead national and international pharmacy groups and has founded a non-profit organization on pharmacy ethics. The writing skills she learned from her English teachers like Mrs. Alice Davis and Ms. Dorothy Yeatman remain with her every time she puts her pen to paper to write pharmacy policies and procedures. She thinks of them with appreciation, especially in view of her life's philosophy. It goes something like this: there is never just one thing that gets you where you are … it's a whole lot of little things adding up over time.

And for her, Alice Davis is one of the biggest little things.

Kelly Hager, Alice's former student who was the web producer for WJZ-TV, remembers Mrs. Davis as a fellow kindred spirit.

Alice's love of literature matched the fire in Kelly's heart for books and words.

Kelly's first memory of Alice wasn't as a high school teacher, but as a summer camp instructor in her elementary school years. Kelly and her best friend signed up for a creative writing class; what they got was Alice Davis teaching them limericks and haikus. As an adult looking back on that summer with her, Kelly marvels at her patience for teaching poetry to fourth graders.

Her best memory of Alice comes later, when she was a teenager in Mrs. Davis's AP English class. Although Kelly had a singular focus — do well and do not disappoint her — she was still a teenager. One day, she had her head down on her desk, listening but not watching. Mrs. Davis noticed and lamented to the class, "Kelly, if you were a horse, I'd have to shoot you." The sarcasm in her quick, dry wit landed exactly on target and cemented a memory in which Kelly can still hear her voice. She laughs every time she thinks about it.

Today, Kelly Hager works in international publishing and is an established book reviewer. Authors, literary agents, and publishing houses send her advanced reader copies of books in the hopes she'll like the work. She's even reviewed the books of a few *New York Times* best selling authors, and has nearly 2,000 followers on her book blog. All for the love of books, a fire once stoked by her old English teacher who loved reading in equal measure.

And that's the hook for Kelly. She remembers a teacher who was tough but kind, smart yet self-effacing, and always demanding the best without actually demanding anything at all. Beyond the vocabulary journals and the terrible news reports which came later, Kelly remembers Alice Davis as a woman who inspired her, challenged her, and nurtured her love of the written word.

For Kelly Hager, Alice mattered.

In the fall of 2000, Brooks Williams entered Alice Davis's class-room as a quiet student who loved to read. When she gave them a list of books and told them to choose their reading assignments, his heart leaped when he saw the first two J.R. Tolkien *Lord of the Rings* books on the list. In Alice he saw a reflection of himself: there was always a stack of books on her desk and on her shelves. *So many books, so little time.* She assigned them to write an essay after reading a poem about a couple of cats who did not understand the finality of death. To the class, she lamented that when she died, her greatest regret would be all the good books she never had a chance to read.

This was the first thing Brooks thought about when he heard she was gone. That, and how glad she had been to see him when he returned for a visit after graduation. She had been the only teacher he sought out.

While Alice may have nurtured his love of books, she also gave him something else he would discover later — his own teaching style. Brooks admired Alice because she knew her material and her kids knew she knew her material. Her delivery was encapsulated in these clever flashes of wit, albeit sometimes her zingers would go right over the head of the kid targeted by her sarcastic barbs. But her commentary never went over Brooks's head. He always understood, perhaps especially since he was never on the receiving end of her playful wrath. He loved the brilliance of her intelligence and her laugh and the way she could size up any situation or student and in doing so, figure out exactly how to connect with them. Alice's style resonated with him.

Brooks Williams became a math teacher and a drama instructor, teaching middle school students. He finds himself emulating her type of humor, dry with a touch of sarcasm yet easy enough as to not be offensive or irritating to the very students he is trying to engage. She was a true professional: she stood tall at the front of the classroom and never goofed off. Brooks is admittedly more laid back and tends to crack a few more jokes than she would have allowed herself. In theater, Brooks loves to see the students take on roles and flourish with words and play. Just like Alice, he finds great delight in seeing literature take center stage and come alive for young people.

When he stands in front of his students, whether in the classroom or in the drama club, he often thinks of Alice.

In 2011, Kelly Hughes Roberts was working on her first book. It was about two orphans in Italy who lose their parents in a terrible accident and must risk their lives to find a place of their own. The lesson: love triumphs over adversity. The story was inspired by a trip to Tuscany, but the confidence to write it came years earlier when she was a student in Mrs. Davis's classroom.

Kelly had always loved to write, and being in Mrs. Davis's English class was like a door opening to a world in which she could flourish and thrive. She saw great passion in her teacher for literature and writing and that passion caught Kelly's attention. *She is just like me*, Kelly thought, and so she wrote and wrote and started to believe in her words because Alice Davis believed in them. After all, it is easy to believe in yourself when someone you respect does too.

A year and four days after Alice's funeral, Kelly Hughes Roberts published her first young adult fiction novel titled *The Road to Chianti*. There was a bittersweet moment when Kelly realized her old English teacher, Alice Davis, would never share in the happiness of this publishing moment with her. It stung … Alice was a key figure in Kelly's early writing foundation and now she was a reason for Kelly to continue on the path. In the years since, Kelly has written three more books and often thinks of Alice when she puts her pen to the paper.

There are other stories, too. One girl didn't have any money for a prom dress so Alice bought a gown for her. Alice, who didn't even attend her own prom, made sure this young girl could.

There was a young man who did odd jobs around the classroom for Alice. He didn't have family or financial support and Alice took him under her wing, even offering him money to do a little work at her house and arranged for him to meet a recruiter to go over his post-high school options. The night of Alice's memorial service at Parkside, he wept.

Another young girl had moved out of her parent's home just before her senior year. She blew off the senior thesis, but Alice knew she would not graduate if she didn't do it. Instead of failing her, Alice gave her extra work to make up the grade. The young girl saw her chance and didn't waste it: she worked day and night on the assignments and was able to graduate on time. Without Alice, she wouldn't have.

Stories like these are the reason why Alice was named Teacher of the Year for Wicomico County in 2000. She cared for us, always willing to help, especially those of us who also felt abnormal or troubled, rejected or lost. She was wholly committed to being a teacher, an aspiration that is more identity and a calling than it is a profession. Alice gave us the best of herself and we are better for it.

And then there is me.

After I left Parkside High School, I headed off to Washington College in Chestertown, Maryland. Everything I had come to love in Mrs. Davis's class — reading, literature, composition — was laid out before me like a giant buffet: Shakespeare, the Harlem

Renaissance, Victorian literature, the modernist movement, poetry studies, fiction writing — and my saving grace, creative non-fiction. I majored in English and minored in Creative Writing, and for my senior thesis, I put together a collection of short stories about the Eastern Shore and submitted it to the Sophie Kerr Prize committee in April 2001. The Sophie Kerr prize was one of the main reasons I had chosen Washington College. It is the largest undergraduate literary award in country. In 2000, the year before I was set to graduate, the winner was Christine Lincoln, who inked a major book deal with Random House and appeared on Oprah. Reminiscent of Alice's class, I worked at a fever pitch under the tutelage of two professors I admired. The entire year was a dream: how many young writers get to spend a year writing a book? I made myself a vow: *when I turn in my thesis, it will be the best work I can do. It may not be enough for the prize, but I will know I gave the best of me.* That was my pledge and I stuck to it.

At graduation in May 2001, the name called out for the prize was mine. I could not believe it. I was stunned. I just sat there, unable to move. Someone sitting next to me grabbed my arm and said, "Hey! That's you!" That was the moment I burst into tears. When I walked up to accept the award, the president of the college handed me a check for $62,000. All I could do was ask him for a hug.

The clock began ticking immediately on my proverbial fifteen minutes of fame. *The Baltimore Sun*, the AP, even *The Washington Post* ran a few articles on me. Back on the Eastern Shore, the local newspaper and television stations began calling. (Oprah did not.) But before I could handle any of that, there was someone else who had to know first.

Within hours of winning the prize, I was standing in my mother's kitchen. I flicked through the pages of the phone book. My hands were shaking as I dialed the number.

"Hello?" It was her.

"Mrs. Davis, I won! I won the Sophie Kerr Prize!"

I wish I could remember everything we said that night, but what I do remember is that she was happy. She laughed. She congratulated me and told me she knew I could do it.

She told me she was proud of me.

As a writer, there have been two great moments of pen-to-paper achievement in my life — the Old Home Prize and the Sophie Kerr Prize — and Alice Davis was there for both of them.

This is how I know that with each word I write, she is close.

•   •   •   •   •

Epilogue

This book was the hardest thing I've ever written.

On the edge of my writing desk sits the Perrine Literature textbook Alice gave me at the end of my senior year. The thick strips of masking tape holding the spine together are now as brittle as parchment paper. Bookmarking the page where Willa Cather begins to tell "Paul's Story" is a small envelope addressed to me and postmarked April 21st, 2006. The return address is a post office box in Allen, Maryland. Inside the envelope is a card, a thank you note for speaking to her students at the National Honor Society "Straight A" reception. The front of the card is emblazened with the Parkside crest. This the last correspondence I have from Alice Davis.

The contents of the card are simple. She apologizes for the note being late; she thanks me for taking the time to speak to the kids; she tells me it was good to see me and catch up. The last line is straight out of a teacher's brain, something she could have written in a student's yearbook: "You are very special and talented and I know you will continue to do well in the future." Maybe it's just a note, but to me, it's a treasure … one last little reminder of her.

When I was a teenager, I put Alice on a pedestal because I respected and admired her. She could do no wrong in my eyes. I thought she had figured out how to be perfect at everything. As I got older and a touch wiser, I realized no one is perfect. We all slip on masks for the world at large. Maybe Alice was just better at that than most. Over the course of writing this book, I realized putting Alice on that pedestal was a disservice to her. She was human after all, just like me, just like you, and just as prone to mistakes and faults. This was a revelation — seeing her in the full, bright light of day instead of the narrow spotlight I had once cast on her. Now, I cannot help but wonder if we are all best loved when we are the most seen.

I sit here, at my desk, staring at that textbook, and I have a deeper, more profound understanding of who she was. Even though Alice now belongs to our memories, she continues to teach me, to challenge me. I think of her often. As I write these final words, I know I will always sense her standing just over my shoulder, appraising my work and holding me accountable to do the best I can. Always.

And that is the greater treasure for me to keep close.

Additional Book Notes

The CNN link referenced in the Author's Note is no longer available as of the publication of this book. I reached out for help but wasn't able to retrieve it prior to publication of this book.

The *Revenge of the Jedi* poster mentioned in Part II is not a typo. The title of the movie was changed to *Return of the Jedi*; however, I have a photograph of her room taken on May 16, 1997 and the poster in her room was absolutely one for *Revenge of the Jedi*.

With regard to Jessica Cordrey, the Maryland Judiciary Case Search shows two cases related to drug charges - 4H00047779 for June 24, 2008 and 3H00049563 for December 21, 2008. In the case information for both dates, the defendant's information is listed as P.O. Box 144 in Allen, MD. This is also the same P.O. Box number Alice and Jess Davis used.

The section "The Manner of Death" was based on the specific, physical findings from the autopsy report. The medical examiner **did not give an opinion** as to how or when these injuries occured, only that they were present. The scene, as written, *is my conclusion* and what I believe happened. There were multiple fractures, some with and some without presence of hemorrhage. The lack of hemorrhage points to those fractures occuring post-mortem.

Domestic Violence Resources

If you or someone you know needs help, then please check out the following organizations:

The National Domestic Violence Hotline
(800) 799-7233
(800) 787-3224 (TTY)
www.thehotline.org

Maryland Network Against Domestic Violence
24-Hour Hotline: (800) 634-3577
www.mnadv.org

Delaware Coalition Against Domestic Violence
(800) 701-0456
www.dcadv.org

Eastern Shore Coalition Against Domestic Violence
(757) 787-1329
www.escadv.org

Life Crisis Center
(410) 749-4357
www.lifecrisiscenter.org

National Coalition Against Domestic Violence
www.ncadv.org/resources

Works Cited

Chasing Alice was a long, long labor of love. It took more than six years and countless hours of research, writing, and revision. The amount of research materials I gathered for this project was massive. There were personal interviews, emails, Facebook messages and posts, books, newspaper articles, online searches, police files, and more. Paper, digitial, audio: you name it and I've got it here in the mountains of files I have gathered. In this section, I have done my best to provide an outline of the resources I used.

Primary Sources

For this book, I filed two Freedom of Information Act/Public Information Act requests with the Wicomico County Sheriff's Department to obtain the police records regarding the murder of Alice Davis and the suicide of Jess Davis. The FOIA/PIA records included but are not limited to: crime scene photographs, officer incident reports and supplements, tip sheets, the 2009 burglary report, evidence logs, search warrants, missing persons report, photo lineups, timeline data, images from survelliance videos, and miscellaneous notes and summaries made by investigating parties.

Additionally, I requested Alice's autopsy and toxicology reports from the Office of the Chief Medical Examiner and a copy of her Will from the local court system.

Other primary sources I used include personal writings from Clarence "Casey" Parsons as well as my own personal recollections, high school memorabilia, letters, documents, online posts, and photographs.

Databases

The Maryland Judiciary Case Search was an early source of important information, especially regarding Jess Davis. This includes his worker's compensation cases, civil disputes, and other charges as well as information about Jessica Pamela Cordrey.

I used the database newspapers.com to find many of the newspaper articles I read for this book. I have listed the most important ones in the selected bibliography below. I also used drugs.com to research several of the medications prescribed to both Alice and Jess.

Wikipedia was a quick search tool that I often used as an initial starting point. Searches included but are not limited to: Allen, Maryland; Asbury Methodist Episcopal Church (Allen, Maryland); Bennett's Adventure; Bounds Lott; Battle of Okinawa; Battle of Midway; *USS Russell* (DD-414); *USS Frank Knox* (DD-742); Childhood absence epilepsy; Parkside High School; Tyaskin, Maryland; Maryland locations by per capita income; Fruitland, Maryland; National Crime Information Center; History of Psychopathy; Theophrastus, Philippe Pinel; Hurricane Irene; Mason-Dixon Line, Psychopathy Checklist, Robert D. Hare, antisocial personality disorder, Gary Dourdan, Nicholas Cage, and focal segmented glomerulosclerosis (FSGS).

Interviews & Correspondences

Blades, Chastity. *Personal interview*. 9 Sept. 2015.

Bennett, Cindy. *Personal interview plus follow up correspondence*. 30 July 2015.

Carey, Marisa. *Personal interview*. 14 Nov. 2015

Collier, Matthew. *Personal interview plus follow up correspondence.* 14 Nov. 2018

Collins, Anne. P*ersonal interview plus follow up correspondence.* 31 May 2018.

Corbin, Tyron. *Personal interview.* 17 Jan. 2019

Dallam, Colleen. *Personal interview.* 29 June 2015.

Dashiell, Gale Glasgow. *Personal interview plus follow up correspondence.* 30 Jan. 2016.

Fowler, Jacki. *Personal correspondence.* 2017 & 2019.

Hager, Kelly. *Personal interview plus follow up correspondence.* 10 June 2018.

Hitch, Ellen Malone. *Personal interview.* 6 Feb. 2018.

Kiviat, Barbara. *Personal correspondence.* 2011.

Leikach, Dixie White. *Personal interview.* 28 September 2019.

Lewis, Michael. *Personal interview.* 30 July 2015.

Lopez, Lori. P*ersonal interview plus follow up correspondence.* 20 January 2019.

Metzger, Sabrina. *Personal interview.* 21 Sept. 2015.

Neville, Bill. *Personal interview.* 5 April 2016.

Neville, Dawn. *Personal interview.* 5 April 2016.

Orme, Aimee. *Personal interview plus follow up correspondence.* 27 February 2020.

Rives, Ann Lawrence. *Personal correspondence.* 2011.

Roberts, Kelly Hughes. *Personal correspondence.* 2011.

Shivers, George. *Personal correspondence.* 2015, 2020.

Slocum, Patricia. *Personal interview.* 14 Aug. 2015.

Stauffer, Micah. *Personal interview.* 21 Feb. 2020.

Thress, Carl. *Personal interview.* 19 Dec. 2018.

Tilghman, Barrie Parsons. *Personal interviews plus follow up correspondence.* 1 July 2015 and 18 Aug. 2015.

Vandervoordt, Tiffany Hoke. *Personal correspondence.* 2011.

Williams, Brooks. *Personal interview.* 16 Jan. 2019.

Select Bibliography
(Articles, Books, and Online Sources)

"Alice (Davis) Parsons's Obituary." *legacy.com*, 2 Oct. 2011, www.legacy.com/obituaries/delmarvanow/obituary.aspx?n=alice-parsons-davis&pid=153897344&fhid=2204. (Information pulled from *Delmarva Now.*)

"Alice E Davis-55, Missing-Maryland-9/6/11." *www.justiceforchandra.com*, 8 Sept. 2011, www.justiceforchandra.com/forums/viewtopic.php?t=4884&highlight=alice+davis.

"Alice Parsons Weds Mr. Davis." *The Daily Times*, 30 Aug. 1985, www.newspapers.com. Accessed 24 Sept. 2017.

American Psychiatric Association. *Diagnostic and Statistical Manual of Mental Disorders : DSM-5.* Arlington, Va., American Psychiatric Association, 2013.

Augenstein, Neal. "Death Investigation Complete for Md. Man Who Killed Self before Murder Trial." *WTOP,* 7 Feb. 2019, wtop.com/local/2019/02/death-investigation-complete-for-md-man-who-killed-self-before-murder-trial/.

Bonn, Scott. "The Differences Between Psychopaths and Sociopaths." *Psychology Today,* 2018, www.psychologytoday.com/us/blog/wicked-deeds/201801/the-differences-between-psychopaths-and-sociopaths.

Boykin, Sharahn D. "Body Identified as Teacher." *The Daily Times,* 13 Sept. 2011, www.newspapers.com. Accessed 25 Sept. 2017.

---. "Foul Play Suspected in Missing Teacher Probe." *The Daily Times,* 8 Sept. 2011, www.newspapers.com. Accessed 25 Sept. 2017.

---. "Police Conclude Davis Case." *The Daily Times,* 16 Sept. 2011, www.newspapers.com. Accessed 25 Sept. 2017.

---. "Questions Linger after Husband's Suicide." *The Daily Times,* 9 Sept. 2011, www.newspapers.com. Accessed 25 Sept. 2017.

---. "Search Continues for Teacher." *The Daily Times,* 10 Sept. 2011, www.newspapers.com. Accessed 25 Sept. 2017.

---. "Teacher Died of Blunt Force Trauma." *The Daily Times,* 15 Sept. 2011, www.newspapers.com. Accessed 25 Sept. 2017.

Brunvand, Jan Harold. *Too Good to Be True : The Colossal Book of Urban Legends.* New York ; London, W. W. Norton & Company, 2014. eText ISBN: 9780393104165.

Community Foundation of the Eastern Shore. "SCHOLARSHIPS." www.cfes.org/scholarships.

Culvyhouse, Henry. "Wicomico Bureau of Investigations Disbanded." *The Daily Times*, 23 Jan. 2017.

Fowler, Stephanie. "Life With Louise: A Kidney Transplant (Love) Story." *Medium*, 9 Mar. 2017, medium.com/@stephaniefowler/ life-with-louise-a-kidney-transplant-love-story-5cf0ea7a278d.

Grohol, John M., et al. "Differences Between a Psychopath vs Sociopath." *Psychcentral.com*, 12 Feb. 2015, psychcentral.com/blog/ archives/2015/02/12/differences-between-a-psychopath-vs-sociopath/.

Hamrick, Terri. "Domestic Violence Awareness Month: What a Week without Domestic Abuse Would Look Like." *USA TODAY*, Treasure Coast Newspapers, 26 Oct. 2019, www.usatoday.com/ story/opinion/2019/10/26/domestic-violence-statistics-women-abuse-pregnancy-column/4081930002/.

"History | Domestic Violence Advocates | National Domestic Violence Hotline." *The National Domestic Violence Hotline*, www.thehotline. org/about-the-hotline/history-domestic-violence-advocates-2/.

Holland, Earl. "Peers Salute Davis' Energy." *The Daily Times*, 6 Oct. 2011, www.newspapers.com. Accessed 25 Sept. 2017.

Huecker, Martin R, and William Smock. "Domestic Violence." *nih. gov*, StatPearls Publishing, 2 May 2019, www.ncbi.nlm.nih.gov/ books/NBK499891/.

"Index Files, Page 359." *Allen Historical Society*, www. allenhistoricalsociety.org/index_files/Page359.htm. *(This site is no longer active.)*

Jiang, Weixiong, et al. "Reduced White Matter Integrity in Antisocial Personality Disorder: A Diffusion Tensor Imaging Study." *Scientific Reports*, vol. 7, no. 1, 22 Feb. 2017, www.ncbi.nlm.nih. gov/pmc/articles/PMC5320449/

Judge, Phoebe. "Money Tree." *Criminal.* Episode 51. Radiotopia. 23 Sept. 2016. thisiscriminal.com/episode-51-money-tree-8-23-2016/

---. "The Checklist." *Criminal.* Episode 52. Radiotopia. 7 Oct. 2016. thisiscriminal.com/episode-52-the-checklist/

Junkin, Vanessa. "Plank Remembered 20 Years Later." *The Daily Times*, 15 Oct. 2015, www.delmarvanow. com/story/news/local/maryland/2015/10/15/ eddie-plank-somerset-county-murder/73973798/.

Lake, Sarah. "Crime, Controversy, Growth, Community: Top 10 Stories of 2011." *The Daily Times*, 31 Dec. 2011, www.newspapers. com. Accessed 25 Sept. 2017.

Lama, Dalai. "Just as Ripples Spread out When a Single Pebble Is Dropped into Water, the Actions of Individuals Can Have Far-Reaching Effects." @DalaiLama, 10 May 2013, twitter.com/ DalaiLama/status/332790603966476288.

Lohr, David. "UPDATE: Maryland School Teacher Missing, Husband Dead From Apparent Self-Inflicted Wound." *HuffPost*, 7 Sept. 2011, www.huffpost.com/entry/ alice-davis-missing-maryland-school-teacher_n_952797.

McKinney, Calum. "Missing Woman's Car Found." *The Daily Times*, 7 Sept. 2011, www.newspapers.com. Accessed 25 Sept. 2017.

Morse, Dan. "A Murder Suspect Allegedly Lured His Pregnant Girlfriend to a Remote Field. Prosecutors Want Jurors to See It." *Washington Post*, 23 Aug. 2018, www.washingtonpost.com/local/public-safety/a-murder-suspect-allegedly-lured-his-pregnant-girlfriend-to-a-remote-field-prosecutors-want-jurors-to-see-it/2018/08/23/bd395388-a6bf-11e8-8fac-12e98c13528d_story.html.

"National Register Properties in Maryland." mht.maryland.gov, Department of Planning, Maryland Historical Trust, mht.maryland.gov/nr/NRCountyList.aspx?FROM=NRPickCounty.aspx&COUNTY=Wicomico. Site copyright 2003-2018.

NephCure Kidney International. "Focal Segmental Glomerulosclerosis (FSGS)." nephcure.org, 2018, nephcure.org/livingwithkidneydisease/understanding-glomerular-disease/understanding-fsgs/. Accessed 6 Dec. 2019.

Ng, Christina. "Video: Missing Maryland Teacher's Husband Commits Suicide." *ABC News*, 8 Sept. 2011, abcnews.go.com/US/video/missing-maryland-teachers-husband-commits-suicide-14473719.

NORD (National Organization for Rare Disorders). "Focal Segmental Glomerulosclerosis." rarediseases.org, rarediseases.org/rare-diseases/focal-segmental-glomerulosclerosis/.

NPR. "Does A Psychopath Who Kills Get To Use The Insanity Defense?" 3 Aug. 2016, www.npr.org/sections/health-shots/2016/08/03/486669552/does-a-psychopath-who-kills-get-to-use-the-insanity-defense.

"Old Home Prize Essay Collection." Edward H. Nabb Research Center Finding Aid Portal, Salisbury University, libapps.salisbury.edu/nabb-archives/finding-aid.php?id=1553.

Our View / Editorial. "A Community's Tale of Horror." *The Daily Times*, 14 Sept. 2011, www.newspapers.com. Accessed 25 Sept. 2017.

Pandav, Jillian. "His name was Generro Sanchez." *Court Junkie*. Episode 64. PodcastOne. 10 Dec. 2018. courtjunkie.libsyn.com/ ep-64-his-name-was-generro-sanchez

Parker, Susan. "February Is Time for Romance." *The Daily Times*, 11 Feb. 1992, www.newspapers.com. Accessed 24 Sept. 2017.

Robinson, Kara Mayer. "Sociopath vs. Psychopath: What's the Difference?" *WebMD*, 23 Feb. 2015, www.webmd.com/ mental-health/features/sociopath-psychopath-difference#1.

Saywell, Melissa. "'Macbeth' Viewing Enhances Studies." *The Daily Times*, 29 Apr. 1997, www.newspapers.com. Accessed 24 Sept. 2017.

Schulz, Kathryn. "Dead Certainty: How 'Making A Murderer Goes Wrong.'" *New Yorker*, 25 Jan. 2016, www.newyorker.com/ magazine/2016/01/25/dead-certainty.

Shivers, George. *Changing Times: Chronicle of Allen, Maryland, An Eastern Shore Village*. Baltimore, Maryland, Gateway Press, 1998. Publication sponsored by the Allen Historical Society.

Staff Reports / News Service Reports. "Hurricane Irene Death Toll Rises to at Least 44." *msnbc.com*, 30 Aug. 2011, www.nbcnews. com/id/44314551/ns/weather/t/hurricane-irene-death-toll-rises- least/#.XqNIIS-ZPOT.

"Statistics | The National Domestic Violence Hotline." *The National Domestic Violence Hotline*, 2018, www.thehotline.org/resources/ statistics/.

Stout, Martha. *The Sociopath next Door : The Ruthless versus the Rest of Us.* New York, Broadway Books, 2005.

"Sussex County Assesses the Damage in Wake of Hurricane Irene | Sussex County." 8 Aug. 2011, sussexcountyde.gov/news/sussex-county-assesses-damage-wake-hurricane-irene.

The Riverside Shakespeare. edited by G. Blakemore Evans and J. J. M. Tobin, Second ed., New York, NY, Houghton Mifflin Company, 1997.

Thress, Carl. "In Memory of Alice Davis." *[Fort]Thress*, 13 Sept. 2011, 4thress.com/blog/In_Memory_of_Alice_Davis.html.

Van Sant, Peter. "The Ultimatum." *48 Hours.* CBS, 8 Aug. 2015, www.cbsnews.com/news/48-hours-did-an-ultimatum-lead-to-the-murder-of-vanessa-mintz/.

WBOC. "Police Conclude Wicomico Co. Woman Murdered by Husband." 15 Sept. 2011, www.wboc.com/story/15472694/cause-of-death-determined-for-wicomico-county-woman. Accessed 31 Dec. 2017.

---. "Services Set for Slain Wicomico County Teacher." 20 Sept. 2011, www.wboc.com/story/15506726/alice-davis-family.

---. "Update: Wicomico County Woman's Death Ruled Homicide." 14 Sept. 2011, www.wboc.com/story/15459880/cause-of-death-determined-for-wicomico-county-woman.

When Men Murder Women: An Analysis of 2011 Homicide Data Females Murdered by Males in Single Victim/Single Offender Incidents. Violence Policy Center, Sept. 2013.

Williams, Aaron. "Sweetwater and Adam Corolla." *Beer Guys Radio.* Episode 20. 12 May 2016. beerguysradio.com/2016/05/12/episode-20-show-preview-sweetwater-carolla/

Willis, Dail. "2 Charged in Slaying of State Trooper." *The Baltimore Sun,* 19 Oct. 1995, www.newspapers.com. Accessed 24 Sept. 2017.

About The Author

Stephanie L. Fowler is a graduate of Washington College in Chestertown, Maryland and the 2001 recipient of the Sophie Kerr Prize, the largest undergraduate literary award in the country. She won the prize for a collection of creative non-fiction short stories written about the Delmarva Peninsula. That collection, *Crossings*, eventually became her first book, published in May 2008.

Since then she has continued to write articles, short stories, essays, and memoir pieces for outlets such as *She Writes: Visions and Voices of Seaside Scribes*, *Coastal Style*, *Medium*, and *One True Thing*. She was a 2016 Light of Literacy award winner and she serves as the president of the Lower Eastern Shore chapter of the Maryland Writers Association. She has been a judge for several regional writing contests and co-hosts a writing podcast called *So, What's Your Story?*

In May 2013, she opened Salt Water Media, an independent self-publishing company, in downtown Berlin, Maryland. Her experience with self-publishing and her passion for writing inspired her to help other writers and authors bring their works to life.

Chasing Alice is her second book and she is currently working on her next project.

A born and bred Marylander, she now lives in southern coastal Delaware with her wife, Patty, and their dog, Lima.